CONQUER YOUR FEAR OF WATER

A REVOLUTIONARY WAY TO LEARN TO SWIM WITHOUT EVER FEELING AFRAID

Melon Dash

For my father,
Dr. William C. Dash, Physicist,
who paved the way for me

This comprehensive guide provides a complete program of new lessons for adults to overcome fear of water and learn to swim on their own. Instructors will elevate their qualification to teach fearful adults.

This book is a revision of *Conquer Your Fear of Water, An Innovative Self Discovery Course in Swimming* (2006). Bearing a new cover and subtitle, it replaces many line drawings with photographs, provides knowledge acquired since the first printing and new illumination about how fear heals. It clarifies several lessons, answers readers' questions, and introduces a new invention for learning to float.

For more about Dash's books, classes, and instructor trainings, visit:
miracleswimming.com
5CirclesTeachingMethod.com and
melondash.com.

Miracle Swimming and The 5 Circles logo are registered trademarks.

I asked myself, "How does fear work?"
The answer came as a diagram on two
occasions in a week of 1983.
On the second occasion, I knew I had it.
The release of lifelong fear by thousands of adult students
and my entire career have resulted
from The 5 Circles. It cannot fail.

BROOKLYN
WRITERS PRESS

Published in New York City by the Brooklyn Writers Press,
an imprint of the Brooklyn Writers Project, LLC.

www.brooklynwriterspress.com

TITLE: Conquer Your Fear of Water
A Revolutionary Way to Learn to Swim Without Ever Feeling Afraid

Illustration by Michelle Becker
Back cover bio photograph by Barbara Banks

ISBN: 978-1-7340973-0-6 (paperback)
ISBN: 978-1-9529911-9-6 (e-book)
ISBN: 978-0-9821081-0-9 (paperback color version)

Library of Congress Catalog Card Number: 2019914998

2nd Edition

PRAISE FOR
CONQUER YOUR FEAR OF WATER

Your methods truly had a miraculous impact on me. My newfound confidence in water has opened doors that I thought would always remain shut. —Rich Kennedy, Manager

As a 60 year old that had tried to learn to swim, this book was a godsend. My situation was summed up in her opening line "something made you afraid of the water." ... I have accomplished more in 12 hours than I did with five years of conventional lessons. —Gary Hayes, Amazon.com reviewer

I learned from your book that my fear of water was a fear of losing control of myself...and now I've just passed the SCUBA open water and written exams. I owe this to you. —Maria Mendoza

This book is a master class. My sincere thanks for writing to us in a manner that gave us confidence. —Amit Gupta

I was about to say, "To hell with swimming!" when I read this book. And thank goodness I did.... Read this book slowly. Absorb each lesson. Dash says it's guaranteed to work and she's right. If you're planning to take swimming lessons, read this before you take a single one. —Piano Player, Amazon.com reviewer

You really can learn this from reading a book. I was doubtful, but it's so complete! This is something that's always been there, but everyone has overlooked it. Nobody ever said it this way. —Suzanne Marthins

I'm an American Red Cross certified instructor and aquatic facility supervisor. Your book has completely turned my focus and teaching methods around. I am now a more effective and compassionate instructor. —Jane Bosse

Dash is onto something big. Her system has affected the way I work with some of my clients. —Nancy Merz, Psychotherapist

I really appreciate the writing style of Ms Dash, how she tells it like it is. It's ok to be afraid of the water. I highly recommend this book and wish I had had it sooner. —Chuck, Amazon.com reviewer

As a college student, Melon identified something that was wrong with the way adults were being taught to swim. She developed a system to teach afraid adults that has set the bar high for every aquatic agency and/or swim instructor—to visit their methods and make some adjustments to meet the needs of adults who have fear of water. —Sue Nelson, USA Swimming

As an American Red Cross Swimming Instructor Trainer for thirty years, I have trained hundreds of instructors. A large, essential portion of the learning process is missing for adults who are afraid in water. Water Safety would reach new heights if this book were used by swim instructors everywhere. It should start defining "learn to swim" the way this book does. —Judy Lemke

This book has more useful information about learning to swim than all the beginning swim classes I've taken in my whole life, combined. I've taken a lot of classes. —Deborah Kemper, Travel Writer

This method cannot and does not fail. —Mary Alice Yund, Chemist

This book is about healing fear. Melon Dash knows how to heal those hobbled by fear of water, deep or shallow, and bring the joy of swimming to all. —Cynthia Tuttelman, M.D.

How does Melon teach people to overcome their fear in water, you ask? The most enjoyable, inspiring, and loving way you could possibly imagine. —Anonymous

Infallible. —John Sitaras

TABLE OF CONTENTS

FOREWORD

Thirsty to learn to swim but feeling afraid? Have some Melonade!

Melon will one day be revered as the first person to clearly explain what many people are missing in everyday swimming lessons. Her longtime emphasis on swimming students' self-reliance in water by learning how to rest has been pivotal, as versions of this same message are now saving lives at sea worldwide.

This book began a monumental improvement in the world of safer swimming instruction because Melon was so doggedly unafraid to ask, honour and support how learners really feel.

Melon's work makes complete sense. This do-it-yourself book repeatedly rises to the top of my list for its clarity and for allowing learners to be themselves. She will not tell you to squash your feelings and relax!

I wish you great fun on your quest to learn to swim or to help others learn. If you give yourself time to unfurl what Melon has to say you will learn to swim in the truest sense of the word.

Andie Andrews
Aquatic Specialist
United Kingdom
Board Member, Lifesaving Foundation

PREFACE

WHAT IS KNOWING HOW TO SWIM?

Let's say you're at a hotel. As you walk to the restaurant, you pass the pool where four people in the deep end are chatting and treading. When you return from your meal, they're still in the same spot. Would you say these people can swim? You didn't see them swimming laps.

If a family rents a houseboat for a week and spends its afternoons in the middle of a lake jumping off the boat, playing tag, lounging on a raft, knocking each other off air mattresses, diving under water to get away from each other, would you say those people could swim? Even if you didn't see them doing strokes?

If you have a friend who swims a mile three times a week in a four-foot-deep pool, but she can't do it in deep water because she'd panic, can she swim?

She can "swim," but she can't swim!

There was a time not long ago—two or three decades—when knowing how to swim meant you were safe in water over your head. You might know strokes too. It was understood that if you weren't comfortable and confident in deep water, you couldn't swim.

In the 1980s and 90s, when swim team coaches became the most influential purveyor of swimming lessons, the main definition of "I can swim" changed from, "I'm safe in deep water" to "I can do freestyle. I can do strokes." Their new lessons didn't allow time to teach students that they float or how the water works with their bodies. Lessons were more concerned with teaching kids how to swim fast.

Adults were taught the same lessons as those given to kids, as they had been for a hundred years. This was never viable for adults who were afraid. The instructional agencies thought that the failure of adults to learn was due to students' not practicing enough. Agencies didn't know their instructors were unequipped to work with fear.

Swimming coaches didn't anticipate a downside of their new curriculum for children. The downside extended to lessons for adults.

It's taken a few decades of living with the fallout of all of this to deduce that in the 1990s or so, many or most swimming lessons stopped teaching safety and stopped requiring safety to "pass the swim test." Instead, they required mechanical skills. The ability to rest and be peaceful in deep water was not tested.

I dare say that in an alarming number of people, it was also not learned.

What is the fallout?

- A shortage of lifeguards: there haven't been enough people who could pass the pre-test to take the training to become a lifeguard. Therefore, the pool of guards is now insufficient.

- Virtually no change in the drowning rate in the past twenty-plus years. One might guess that the drowning rate would have increased noticeably in that time except for the valiant efforts of the new industry of Drowning Prevention which has prevented many deaths.

- Twenty and thirty-somethings who cling to the sides in deep water even though they took swimming lessons and their parents think they can swim.

- Adults and kids who think they can swim, but can't. What could be more unsafe? They try out for swim teams. They say they can swim. They swim from the shallow end toward the deep end and suddenly head for the side at the dropoff. The coach says, "I thought you said you could swim." The 'swimmer' says, "I can, until I get to deep water." The coach says, "I'm sorry, but you don't know how to swim."

- Many adults who quit swimming lessons because the lessons don't meet their needs. Many become discouraged and resign themselves to not swimming: "I guess swimming isn't meant for me."

- People who pass the common swim test without proving that they can rest in deep water; therefore, they haven't shown that they're safe.

- Many people who are afraid in water who believe they simply need to learn to tread water to be safe. This is not possible until they can swim.

This book teaches adults how to be comfortable and safe in water, shallow and deep: to swim. It provides all the ideas, explanations, skills, and steps that are essential to learning comfort and safety. When you've embodied them—when you can swim—you can go on to learn strokes without struggle.

Strokes provide swimming *efficiency*. But safety must come first. It turns out that it's not movement in deep water that makes you safe: it's the ability to remain still inside. One day, this will be the goal of all beginning swimming courses.

Melon Dash, Founder
Miracle Swimming School for Adults, LLC
Sarasota, Florida

INTRODUCTION

I love the water. It's the depth that gets me.
—Giselle

If you know that 2+2 equals 4, and you see the world adding 2+3 or 2+6 or 2+135 and trying to get 4, always coming up with an incorrect answer and basing further calculations on these answers, you might feel as I do, like shouting from the rooftops, "Two plus two is four! I can show you. The rest of your calculations will be correct. Life will be easier!"

For a century, many adults have taken swimming classes that didn't meet them at their level. Their level was "afraid." This stage precedes "Beginning Swimming" lessons but hadn't been identified as a stage until the 1980s. "Afraid" has been treated as insignificant. Instructor trainings have been devoid of tools to address it. But instructors are beginning to learn that "afraid" has its own set of needs and skills. These steps may not be skipped.

Overcoming fear is an intimate process that takes place at your core. It requires slowing down and coming to a full stop. The journey is simple and clear. The process is reliable, predictable, and fun. It just may involve something you never considered before. I hope you'll treat yourself with the utmost respect, compassion, and patience.

By my definition, if you're uncomfortable in water, you're afraid of something. There are no silly reasons for being afraid. An understanding is missing. It makes complete sense to be afraid in water until you know how the water works and how to be in control in it. However, knowing how it works and how to be in control in it have never been systematically taught in beginning swimming classes, to my knowledge. Would anyone expect a five-year-old to learn to read without learning the alphabet first? You must be met at your level, taught the basics, and all your questions must be answered correctly.

Topics in this book are presented as they arise in class. You will come to a new understanding. It will turn your swimming around.

TWO—AN ADULT AFRAID IN WATER—AND TWO— THE INFORMATION IN THIS BOOK—EQUALS FOUR: AN ADULT WHO IS CONFIDENT, SAFE, AND FREE IN WATER AND KNOWS HOW TO REMAIN SAFE. IT WORKS EVERY SINGLE TIME.

It's my wish that in my lifetime, all swim instructors will learn how to teach "2+2=4."

Q.   Why haven't you learned to swim?

A.   Because you weren't comfortable. I hope you'll follow the steps in this book "to a T." *It's about fun!*

PART 1

THE URGENCY TO GET STARTED

Urgency is understandable, but it impedes learning.
Feel the buzz.

Urgency is a desperate sense of wanting to be ahead of where you are. In a few pages, you'll find what happens inside us when we're ahead of ourselves. Be aware of this debilitating state.

Wanting to be somewhere you're not:
your body is on the left. Your attention—you—are on the right.

You may feel like skipping these early pages and going directly to the skills. But understanding the material in the following pages is a critical first step for learning.

How long have you yearned to be free in water? Number of years: _____

For now, please feel the sensation of urgency if you have it—the hurry, internal speed, tension, excitement, wanting-to-get-this-part-over-with—and allow it to be there.

There are times when urgency is a useful thing. Learning to overcome fear and swim is *not* one of those times. When you want to learn, the feeling of urgency helps you get started but it also can tempt you to skip steps. If you are urgent to learn, feel where urgency is in your body and stop reading to experience it *fully now.*

Why stop reading to experience it? Because when you become present to it, it has its first chance to let go. When it lets go, then instead of your attention being focused on the goal, all your attention will be in the present, available for learning. With all your attention available for learning, you cannot fail.

Here are three of the most common statements of adult swimming students.

"I'M AFRAID IN THE DEEP, NOT THE SHALLOW"

Someone who is afraid in deep water but not in the shallow is confident in the shallow because he (or she) can stand up. In other words, he depends on the bottom or the side for his safety. However, he doesn't truly know shallow water. He doesn't *know* how it works with his body. If he did, he'd be free in the deep.

I've taught my class in a pool that was no deeper than five feet and people overcame their fear of deep water. No, those people weren't short!

Do you want to rely on yourself for your safety in the shallow and deep rather than on the bottom or the side? If so, then get to know shallow water. Start at the beginning and skip no steps. It may seem that there are a lot of steps in this book, but they're not what you may think. Besides, many steps are short. I dare say, being in a rush to learn is part of what has kept you from getting to know the water. To learn to swim, you'll need to slow down, feel the water, and get to know it. Doing so is not drudgery, tedious, or something to get past. It's rich and fun. The water is an amazing place. It gives you things you do not yet have.

"I JUST NEED TO LEARN TO BREATHE"

Most people who can do a stroke like freestyle who cannot get air during the stroke are tense and rushed. You won't learn to breathe while you're tense and rushed. People may say they're tense because they can't get air. Guess what? That's probably not the reason. More likely, they don't know the water holds them up. Knowing it holds them up makes all the difference. And if the water truly doesn't hold them up—which is the case for a small percentage of people—then they don't know how to be calm if they sink. A *swimmer* is calm even if he or she is not a floater. When you "know the water," you will be at home and comfortable as a floater or a sinker and be able to get air on your own without effort.

You may be thinking, "She's going to tell me to relax." But no, I would never tell you that.

"I JUST NEED TO LEARN TO TREAD"

Contrary to popular opinion, someone who is fearful in deep water is no-where near ready to learn to tread water. Even if they could muster the move-ments to support their heads above the surface for a few seconds, it would be unsustainable due to fear and exhaustion.

Learning to swim is a different process for adults than you may have thought. I hope you'll take your time and grasp the remarkable teaching of this book.

PART 2

HOW TO KNOW IF YOU'RE AFRAID IN WATER

Some people who are afraid in water know they're afraid, and some don't. Students have said to me, "I'm not sure I'm afraid in water. But I do cling to the sides when I'm in the deep." To me, clinging to the sides in the deep means they're afraid.

Have you been unsuccessful learning how to rest or breathe while swimming? Perhaps you believe it's because you haven't practiced enough or that the instructor didn't have enough teaching experience. Those could be true. Or, it may be that you weren't in control.

If you're not calm in the middle of the deep end of the pool, or swimming out to a raft in a lake and stopping to rest on the way, or at any point between the lawn chair and deep water, this book is written for you. Discomfort and uncertainty are two faces of fear. If you weren't afraid, you wouldn't hesitate to go to the raft—even if you didn't know strokes. If you have wished you could swim, or felt badly that you couldn't, rest assured: it's okay to be afraid in water. And there is a pleasant path out of fear to freedom.

Do you think that just because you can't swim, or you panic in deep water, or you get water in your nose, or you can't open your eyes under water, or you sink, or you can't get a breath, or you didn't pass your swimming test...you weren't born a swimmer? Impossible. You were born with the blueprint to learn to swim, every bit as much as the fastest swimmers in the world were. Soon, you'll know this, as I do.

PART 3

WHAT HAPPENED?

You are not alone.

The same thing happened to everyone who is afraid in water. It happened millions of ways, but there is a common thread among all of them.

Something made you afraid in water. For most people, it was a frightening experience in water. Also, for most people, a parent was afraid in water or "didn't swim." For a few people, the cause of fear is unknown. Virtually always, there was a loss of control. This fear can be healed.

Here is one sample of an early experience of a student who was afraid.

> *"My fear of water began years ago, when as a child, a well-intentioned but uninformed swim teacher pushed me into the deep end of the pool, thinking this would get me to swim. Needless to say, he was mistaken. I went on to become an adult who loved water but never fully enjoyed being in water because I was always nervous and afraid. I've tried other classes since then. But it seemed as though I could never "get" the breathing, my arms and legs refused to work together, and the panic in my belly just wouldn't go away. Plus, the teacher usually wanted me to do things that I didn't feel ready to do. It was awful.*
>
> *The most important lesson Miracle Swimming taught me is that when I take my time, going as slowly as I need to in order to feel safe and comfortable, I learn. I learn without fail, and with great joy."*
>
> —Anonymous

PART 4

WHAT DIDN'T HAPPEN?

Relieve yourself of a burden.
Why learning to swim hasn't worked.
It's not your fault.

After you became afraid, you may or may not have tried to overcome it. What you needed was not what you found, however. Your questions may have gone unanswered. Perhaps you were given misinformation or learning steps that were out of order. The instructors didn't know.

$$2+100 \neq 4$$

Everyone can learn to swim. Yes, you. It's not that you can learn to swim if you grin and bear it. It's not that you can learn to swim if you feel the fear and do it anyway, though that approach has its place elsewhere. It's not that you can learn to swim if you force yourself. It's that you can learn to swim happily, gently, and predictably. There's no mystery about it anymore.

If you've taken swimming lessons before and you haven't learned to swim or to breathe or to be comfortable in water shallow and deep, it's probably because you and the instructor were trying to add 2 and "not 2" to get 4. You were probably trying to add "you" plus "swimming mechanics" to get confidence. They don't add up.

Yes, you can make some progress in conventional "swimming" lessons. But the lessons fall short of what an afraid learner needs. However, if we add your "self" to the full list of sequential steps of learning, it will add up to safety, freedom in water both shallow and deep, comfortable swimming, and skill in preventing panic. If you haven't yet reached your goals, you are like thousands of people worldwide who have asked me, "Will your lessons work for me?" In a word, yes!

Most likely, your instructors and their trainers were unaware that traditional lessons didn't teach people to swim; they taught strokes instead. The distinction had not been made. The safety standards of afraid students were not met. But instructors thought they were doing the right thing.

In order to make all swimming students as safe as they can be, instruction must dive to the depths of what safety really is. It's not simply, "Learn strokes and treading." Safety resides at a level never before, to my knowledge, examined by the swimming and aquatics industries. This book teaches it. The details were discovered in 1983. This new system of keeping yourself safe is the very definition of mindfulness.

It's okay to be afraid in water. In fact, about half of adults in America are. Many say, "I love the water." But put them in deep open water (lakes, oceans) and 64% (158 million adults) are afraid. Put them in water over their heads in a pool, and 46% (114 million) are afraid. Thirty-nine percent are afraid to put their heads under water (Gallup, 1998.) Yet all of them, and you, were born to be swimmers. If someone can swim, he or she is not afraid in deep water.

What is swimming, anyway? Is it perfect strokes, even if done fearfully? Is it going from here to there in water without being able to stop and rest in the middle?

I believe that knowing how to swim is not about doing a perfect stroke... or even knowing strokes at all. My definition of, "I can swim" is confidence that you can rely on yourself for your safety in water over your head and the ability to do so. Confidence in water automatically brings ease in water, the ability tto move from here to there without tiring, being free to play, and having a choice about what to do. It brings a curiosity about deep water: "Is deep water the same as shallow?" And in the answering of that question, a beginning student learns that yes, it is. Only his mind is different in the deep; he "loses" it. And that raises the question, "What shall I do about my mind in deep water?"

In my opinion, and in that of most of my students, if someone can do the crawl stroke in shallow water but not in deep water with confidence, he or she cannot really swim yet. She would say, "I can swim—sort of." To her, the term swimming includes not just mechanics but also the component of confidence. Both are your birthright.

Everyone is born a swimmer. Everyone is born a talker and a walker, a reader and a driver. You weren't born knowing how to do these things. You have the blueprint within you to learn them. You just needed the steps. You learned how to walk and talk beautifully because you didn't skip any steps. You learned to read and drive step by step. You didn't learn to swim because many steps were skipped. But if you skip no steps, it's inevitable that you'll learn.

If you're afraid in water and you're like the six thousand adults that I and my licensees have taught since 1983, you've felt frustrated and confined not to be able to learn to swim. You may have felt embarrassment and shame as well. You have missed opportunities. You want to be free.

If someone is afraid in water, there's an essential ingredient he needs before he can learn swimming mechanics. (When I use "she" or "he," I mean both genders.) If it's not learned, the student won't learn to swim, period. Those people who already have it are the people who learn to swim.

That essential ingredient is control. Despite the fact that swimming has been taught to millions of people without teaching control, the system that was used was not based on universal principles that worked for all students. It has never worked for adults who are afraid, nor does it teach true safety. The millions of students who did learn to swim—i.e., became confident in deep water—were in control. Since instructors believed that everyone was in control, control—and by extension, the ability to learn with their system—was

assumed. It was an incorrect assumption. Therefore, control was never identified as Step 1.

2+2=4
IF YOU DON'T HAVE STEP 1, YOU CAN'T REACH STEP 2

And what is safety? Yes, it can be "no boats driving through the swim area."
But this is not the primary safety you're concerned with. You're concerned
with the safety you'll feel if you're in control of yourself—you know you
won't panic.

Learning safety did not happen. Instructors thought your safety came from
them: "I'm here. You're safe." But it comes from within.

2+2=4
YOU HAVE TO BE IN CONTROL TO LEARN TO SWIM

PART 5

HOW TO FIX IT

Nuts and bolts of overcoming fear.
The steps of learning to swim.
Overcoming fear IS learning to swim.
Fix the problem.

THE TEN FRONTS OF FREEDOM IN WATER

A "front" is a leading edge. In overcoming fear in water, there are ten fronts on which you can make progress toward the goal of freedom in deep water (ten angles from which to approach it). Each is part of the whole picture. When you've reached your limit of what's fun on one front, you can turn to another front and continue to make progress. Progress on one front builds confidence, which enhances your progress on all fronts. Resting often brings up the rear on each front as well. The fronts are (in no particular order):

- Fun, Presence, Control and Internal Speed
- Beliefs
- Face
- Front
- Back
- Vertical
- Propulsion
- Breath
- Water Entries
- Deep Water

For each of these components of learning to swim, there is a sequence of steps that, when followed, takes you to the goal: freedom in that area. The most important front is fun, presence, control, and internal speed. From fun, all the rest are made possible.

This book intersperses all ten fronts throughout the book, the same way Miracle Swimming classes are taught. You'll make a little progress here, then switch to another front and make a little progress there, then switch again and make progress over there. Little by little, predictably and systematically, you grow. Growth happens quickly if you go slowly and skip no steps.

Step 1: 2+2=4

If we know that 2+2=4, and we base our adding of 2+2 on this truth, we will get the correct answer every time. If we add 2+3 or 2+6 trying to get 4, we will never get the correct answer. Everything else based on the incorrect answer will be further afield of the truth.

That is why you should not expect to learn to do freestyle or tread water or breathe if your front float is tense and uncomfortable. A tense front float plus stroke mechanics do not equal a comfortable, viable freestyle.

In learning to swim, the "correct answer" is comfort and control in water, not just the ability to go from here to there with pretty strokes. Once you have comfort and control, learning to go from here to there is automatic and guaranteed.

Historically, the formula of swimming instruction with students who are afraid has been:

A student who is afraid
+ *being taught stroke mechanics*
+ *being asked to keep up with the rest of the class*
+ *no discussion of how students feel*
+ *lack of instruction in how to remain in control*

= a student who is uncomfortable, unsafe in some shallow-water and most deep-water situations, stroking if she's lucky, but not swimming. She is afraid in the deep and does not call herself a swimmer.

The common formula for students who are *not* afraid is the same as above, but the result is a person who is safe in most situations but has no idea what to do if he becomes afraid. He wings it.

To get the correct answer, this sums it up:

a student who is afraid or not afraid

+ *permission to learn at his own pace*

+ *an opportunity to share feelings and thoughts*

+ *learning what's required to stay in control*

+ *satisfactory, correct answers to all his questions*

+ *all the steps of learning to swim in sequence*

_____

= a person who is confident and safe, allowing him to access his natural ability and, without effort or thought, to make up the mechanics on the spot to go from here to there with ease, the same way a child learns to walk.

It has been thought that by learning swimming mechanics an adult would overcome fear. However, stroke mechanics don't help adults overcome their fear. They can make it worse.

SWIMMING MECHANICS HAVE NO MEANING
UNTIL YOU CAN FEEL WHAT'S HAPPENING.

If you're terrified, you can't feel how much the water is doing for you.

2+2=4

MOST ADULTS LEARN TO SWIM TO ADD PEACE OF MIND AND PLEASURE TO THEIR LIVES. SINCE THAT IS THEIR GOAL, PEACE OF MIND AND PLEASURE IN WATER ARE THE MOST IMPORTANT THINGS TO PRACTICE.

It's true that strokes give you control of something: propulsion and speed. Strokes provide efficiency. You can swim faster with them than without them.

However, no stroke and no swimmer—regardless of talent and speed—can out-swim a shark or even a small fish (not that you'll need to, but it seems to be in the back of people's minds). Strokes don't make a person safe.

Millions of adults know how to do a stroke, but they're still afraid in deep water and open water. They're not in control in deep water, so what good will strokes do? You must be in control in deep water in order to learn skills, perform them and rest there. The minimum level of control needed is control over yourself, not over propulsion or speed. All afraid-in-water students I've met agree that they don't feel in control of themselves in deep water.

True or false?

YOU WANT YOUR SAFETY TO COME FROM YOURSELF, NOT FROM THE BOTTOM OR THE SIDE OF THE POOL ...OR STROKES.

By control, I don't mean that you're saying over and over to yourself, "I'm safe. Just do it. You can get there." I mean you can just be yourself in water, perfectly quiet within, and enjoy yourself without doing anything in particular. The water is so different from land that the experience of simply being in water is enough to be interesting, to arouse curiosity, to satisfy. Even if it weren't interesting, it would still be essential to be in control if you wanted to swim and keep yourself safe.

Being in water is bringing your full presence to it. It's being completely "here." Nothing is completely available to you and me unless we're experiencing it while we're completely here. In school when we were children, it was called "applying yourself." Only when we are completely "here" can we receive all that's being given and all that's inherently present. The gifts of being completely here can be mind-blowing. In the case of learning how to be comfortable in the water—pool and ocean—my students have used that very term.

Have you ever "flown off the handle" and later regretted it? Surely, we all have. Flying off the handle is loss of control in an irretrievable way. This is panic, the same as panic in deep water. The solution is the same for both, and it's simple. Naturally, this book is about the panic in water. The solution works for all panic.

When you're in control, you have choices. You can ask yourself, "Would I rather do this, or that?" When we're not in control, we act from a place of survival, habit, or "instincts" that we can't change in the moment. It's almost as though we have no mind. Indeed, when we are in these moments, we have—for all intents and purposes—lost our minds.

2+2=4
WHEN YOU'RE NOT IN CONTROL, YOU DON'T HAVE A CHOICE.

This book illustrates learning: the learning of you, a person, not just a physical body but a non-physical being who fills and controls the body. We use this essential truth of you and me to heal fear and learn to swim. Healing fear and learning to swim are about what you do with your self, not your body. First, learn what to do with your self—be peaceful—and then it's easy to learn what to do with your body—mechanics. Without this fundamental point, you have virtually no chance of becoming free in deep water.

> *Learning to swim is becoming peaceful and competent in water over one's head. Strokes are merely choreography. Choreography makes swimming more efficient. You must learn to swim before you learn to swim swim efficiently.*

2+2=4
IF YOU DON'T HAVE THE CORRECT INFORMATION, YOU HAVE LITTLE CHANCE OF SUCCESS.

Many people learn to swim without ever hearing about or learning the essential non-physical skill of remaining in control. This is fine, until an emergency in water comes up. And when emergencies come up, many swimmers don't know what to do; sometimes good swimmers drown. This is partly because they were never taught the true fundamentals of safety. Most instructors believe fervently that they teach safety. But they were never trained in the true fundamentals of safety themselves. No one was, as far as I know. Most adults in the United States—and the world?— even those who have taken swimming lessons, are not comfortable in deep open water, and therefore they aren't safe. If control in water is taught, the results are more positive than students imagined possible. Students call their experience a miracle.

Please consider letting yourself off the hook for not having learned to swim. When you receive all the pertinent information and learn it, you cannot possibly fail. Not that everyone has to overcome his or her fear with this method, but we have not seen any other teaching that goes straight to the heart of panic-prevention, confidence, and safety. Without those, you can't learn to swim. The amount of confidence you gain, the level of skill you attain, and the degree of challenges you can meet are likely not optimal without this information.

STEP 2: HOW TO STAY IN CONTROL

Where are you? Where is your self? If you were to point to yourself, where would you point? Some people point to their heads. Some point to their hearts. What about you? If a surgeon opened you up there, would she find you? No, she wouldn't find *you*. She'd find bones and tissues but not you. You aren't physical. You have a physical body, but you are non-physical.

We *have* bodies. We *have* feelings. We *have* thoughts. Who is it that has these things? You and I, each a spirit, have them. We are spirit first: the self.

Do you agree that we humans are spiritual beings living in physical bodies in a physical world? It's useful to think of ourselves as energy, or spirit. When we think of ourselves as formless energy or spirit, it gives us a new understanding of our freedom of "movement." I don't mean freedom of physical movement. We understand that we're free to move our limbs if we're able-bodied. I'm referring to our movement as spirit in a body. In other words, how do we move while our bodies are still? Daydreaming is an example.

Your body conforms to physical laws like the law of gravity. Your spirit, however, doesn't conform to physical laws. This must be taken into account in order for teaching and learning to be most effective.

You are the one who controls your body. You are the one with whom instructors must communicate, the one whose trust they must earn, and whose attention they must keep. You must be in control of your self and your body in water. Otherwise, teaching won't work and learning won't happen. If you're afraid you might die, you cannot follow the instructions, "Do this with your arms."

$2+2=4$

ONCE YOU'RE IN CONTROL OF YOURSELF,
YOU CAN THEN BE IN CONTROL OF YOUR BODY.

To get to the bottom of learning, we must understand and address both the non-physical you—which I call you, your self, or spirit—and the body.

When you start a swimming class, you may wonder, "How can I stand to put my face in water? How can I remain safe in deep water?" These must be answered before anyone can expect you to "hear" anything else about swimming.

When using this book, please remain safe and in control in the water by *doing only what you want to do. Never put yourself into a position where you have to do something you don't like or don't want to do.*

It's important to do only that which you want to do because that's the only way we can be sure that you will be present for it. If you do something you don't really want to do, part of you resists what the other part is doing. That means you're divided against yourself. You're not fully "there."

If you aren't fully there, how can you expect yourself to learn? How can anyone else expect you to learn?

> # 2+2=4
> ### YOU MUST BE PRESENT TO LEARN.

You need to enjoy yourself. Don't you owe that to yourself? Being present and having fun are two things that swimming lessons have never required. Students who are afraid are often thinking, "Will the instructor ask me to do something I don't want to do? Will I drown? Am I safe? What if I panic? How will I get air? How will I stand up? Will I make a fool of myself? What if I sink?"

> # 2+2=4
> ### YOU CAN'T LEARN WHAT TO DO WITH YOUR ARMS AND LEGS
> ### IF YOU'RE AFRAID YOU MIGHT NOT LIVE.

What do I mean by being present? I mean "here." You're in control, you know where you are, and you know what you're doing. You're satisfied with how you're handling things. Everyone can learn to swim if they practice the right things. It's fun...so my students have told me for over thirty-five years.

2+2=4

TO REMAIN IN CONTROL OF YOURSELF, YOU MUST KEEP YOURSELF AS A SPIRIT IN YOUR BODY.

Take a moment to absorb what this means.

If you have taken swimming lessons before and worried about your safety, it was impossible to be successful learning mechanics. By learning, I mean embodying the mechanics so that you could use them anytime without thinking.

Here is a diagram of being present. As you come to understand it, you will find that it's the very definition of mindfulness.

Present: You and your body are in the same place. The stick figure represents your body. The circle and the space within it represent you, a spirit. In this situation you'd say, "I feel good."

When you're present, your spirit and your body are in the same space. In the graphic above, the circle and the area within it represent your presence, you as a spirit, your self. In this diagram, you and your body are together. You're "there." You're in control of your body. You feel safe. You're as calm and comfortable as if you were reading the Sunday paper on the couch. In our everyday language, we call this being present, "at home," composed, grounded, centered, together, mindful. You feel poised, quiet, solid, in control, stable, self-contained, peaceful, balanced, open, and comfortable.

Here's a diagram of nervousness: beginning to lose presence. It can happen on land, in water, or anywhere:

Nervous:
You'd say, "I'm nervous, but I'm okay."

In nervousness, you don't feel terrible, but you don't feel good anymore, as you did in the 1st Circle. You're mostly in control, but not completely. In everyday language, we call this, "having cold feet, weak in the knees, a question in the air, buzzing." As a spirit, you aren't completely in your body anymore. You've begun to rise upward through the top of your head.

Here's a diagram of when we've become still more afraid:

Afraid:
"This is not fun. Get me out of here!"

Afraid: we are further out of our bodies. There's little or no presence of us as a spirit in our bodies below the chest. This causes the common knot in the stomach, butterflies in the stomach, and clammy hands and feet. There's less presence of the spirit in the body to keep things stable. We're no longer having fun.

Here's a diagram of us when we're terrified.

**Paralyzed by fear.
"HELP!"**

Your spirit has left your body all the way to your neck. There's no presence of you below the neck. You can't move a muscle. We call this "scared stiff" or "paralyzed by fear." If we're out of the body a little bit further, above the mouth, we're unable to call for help; we can't make a sound or form a word.

Finally, here's a diagram of panic.

**Panic:
Out of it. "Help me get back!"**

We call this "losing it," gone, panicked, not home, out of it, freaked out. "Out" is quite correct. The spirit is out of the body, not permanently, and not completely, but enough for the body to be in danger. There's still a thin thread of energy that connects us to our bodies when we are in panic. If we return to the body, it's not because we're in control of doing so; it just happens.

If, once you return from panic, someone asks you what happened, you would say you don't know. This is because you weren't there to experience it. You left your body first. Someone watching you could tell you what your body did, but you wouldn't remember since you weren't "there."

WHAT IS CONTROL?

It's purposely and habitually keeping yourself, as a spirit, completely in your body.

PANIC PREVENTION

> # 2+2=4
> TO OVERCOME FEAR IN WATER, YOU NEED TO KNOW
> HOW TO REMAIN IN CONTROL AND PREVENT PANIC.

Remaining in control is the key to the door of confidence. It begins with the awareness that you have a choice to stay "here" or leave. The next step is *choosing* to stay here or leave (give up). Once you decide to stay here, the next step is to *feel*. Feeling keeps you in your body. The next step is to follow the instructions that come to you. All of this takes place in less than five seconds.

If we have no choice when certain situations arise, that is, if panic is a habit, then there's no chance to remain in control on purpose. We're in the throes of our habit. Only when we slow down can we have a choice. Without slowing down, there is no learning of panic prevention.

Question: Slow down what?
Answer: Slow down our internal speed: our vibration. You and I have various internal "speeds." When we're calm, our speed is very slow, or still. When we're not calm, our energy moves faster. Our incremental speeds can be called calm, contentedness, interest, fascination, concern, watchfulness, protectiveness, nervousness, fear, struggle, and panic. No doubt, we've all

felt these increments of internal speed. When we're struggling, our energy is moving—vibrating—very fast.

Q: How do I slow down my internal speed, my vibration?
A: By *feeling it and allowing it to be there.*

Q: How can this be fun?
A: By taking it slowly, only doing what's comfortable and taking plenty of rests. The process is deeply rewarding. It's fun, not scary, and it heals fear.

There is no need to go past the 2nd Circle. The 2nd Circle is a warning that it's time to stop and regroup.

Once we slow things down, we have a choice. From the choice not to panic (or even to be uncomfortable) we remain in control. In control, we maintain the highest degree of safety that's possible in the moment.

YOUR VIBRATION OR INTERNAL SPEED

We may think of ourselves as having no input over how fast our internal "speed" is. We may suddenly find ourselves "speeding" and feel stuck there, "rattled."

When you are tense, you're speeding to some degree. You can learn what to do with this speed.

LOCATION, LOCATION, LOCATION

The 5 Circle diagrams represent the main stages we go through when we're in a situation and we become more afraid. However, just because they're typical stages, it doesn't mean they're desirable or required. In fact, they're not helpful. It would be preferable if we could stay in the 1st Circle even when something very frightening is happening.

The Steps of Panic: leaving your body ©M. Dash 1983

If you're chopping vegetables in the kitchen and you cut your finger while thinking about your children driving home in a blizzard, where are you? Are you completely in the kitchen? No. Part of you is in the kitchen and part of you is in the car. You wouldn't say to yourself, "Here's my knife, here's my finger, I'll slice right here." You were not in complete control of your hands or the knife. You couldn't control your body (hands) since you weren't in it.

WHERE YOU ARE RELATIVE TO YOUR BODY

You and I enter, leave, and remain in our bodies at different times of the day. When we're "at home," we're in our bodies, calm and relaxed. We're in our bodies when we feel in control.

If you're sitting at your desk at work daydreaming about being in Hawaii, your body is at your desk, but you are in Hawaii. If someone knocks on your door, the sound brings you back to your desk. If you're reading a book and you have to read the same paragraph three times, your body is in the chair, but you are somewhere else.

We can be "at home," solidly in our bodies. We can be partly in and partly out and cut our finger with a knife. And we can be completely out—when we panic and can't stop ourselves.

Likewise, when we're focused on something that's not happening now, in a fantasy of the future (what if...?) or a memory of the past (I can't let X happen again), *we are in* the future or in the past. We are not here. If you're in the water feeling afraid, you're not completely here; therefore, you're not in control. Don't even think about *learning to swim* in this state. This is when you can easily fly out to the third, fourth, or fifth circles, even if there's no physical danger.

The farther out you go past the 1st Circle, the easier it is to go out even farther. We humans have formed a habit of letting ourselves jump out of the present into the future to "protect ourselves from danger." Sometimes, it's necessary to protect ourselves. At other times, it's not appropriate because there's no danger or because we'd be better off staying here and attending to what our bodies are telling us. They tell us how to be safe...as safe as we can be.

In the not-dangerous times it's useful to keep ourselves in the present, in control. In the dangerous times it's *essential* to keep ourselves in our bodies. Otherwise, we are of no use to our bodies. Perhaps you were of no use to your body once. Don't worry, we all do it at various times in life out of the water!

Because the fundamental act of remaining in control is *remaining in your body*, we can say that being in control is a matter of your location. In your body, you're in control. When you're partly or completely out of your body, you're partly or completely out of control.

Since the fundamental act of remaining safe is about your location as a spirit relative to your body, learning is a spirit event. Obviously, this has nothing to do with religion. It's about the location and movement of you as spirit.

For learning to be optimal, we must take into account our characteristics as spirit. The fact that we are spiritual beings is so ordinary and invisible that it has been overlooked in most teaching. Overcoming fear and learning are spiritual and physical events. First and foremost, overcoming fear is about spirit.

Question: How long does it take to go from the 1st Circle to the 5th?

Answer: No time flat. You can feel fine one moment and in the next moment, panic. You've probably experienced this.

Q: Who's in charge of the circle you're in?

A: Right. *You* are. You may think that *circumstances* cause you to leave your body and go to the next circle. But circumstances are not the cause. It's likely *a belief* you have that's the cause. For example, "I will sink. I might drown." This belief would cause you to leave the 1st Circle. In the past, if you had known *why you must stay* in your body, you would have thought twice about leaving. But you didn't know the importance of your location.

2+2=4

IF YOU DON'T KNOW YOU'RE IN CONTROL OF YOUR LOCATION, YOU AREN'T.

Once we know that moving out of the 1st Circle is what causes us to lose control, we can learn how to remain in the 1st Circle and in control on purpose. This is simple.

WHY WOULD ANYONE LEAVE THE 1ST CIRCLE IF DOING SO WOULD PUT HIM IN DANGER?

Please don't blame yourself; it's a learned response. We learn when we're children to leave the 1st Circle. We leave our bodies when we would rather not feel what's happening. Fear, emotional and physical pain, or any situation you can think of that would be too much to bear is reason enough to leave. A five-year-old being held under water by his playful older brother past the point of fun or safety can either stay in his body and feel extreme discomfort (no air, desperation, possibly rage) or he can leave his body. Who would stay?

Leaving the 1st Circle is an adaptation to pain. Over time, it becomes a habit. When it appears that something is going to feel bad, or we're reminded of something that felt bad, we leave our bodies. No one can be blamed for it. We began doing it long before we knew the consequences: losing control. But this habit can be replaced with a more useful one: the habit of staying here. This is the path to overcoming fear and gaining your freedom in water.

In this book, we will learn first how to be safe and in control, how to stay in the 1st Circle and return to it if you notice you're in the 2nd. We don't go to a higher circle than that. We prevent it. You can be in control enough to prevent it.

When you *know* you're safe, you exert no effort or thought to remain in the 1st Circle. When you're *not sure* you're safe, you need to know how to remain in the 1st Circle and how to get back to it on purpose.

BEING IN CONTROL

If I know that I can't put my feet on the bottom, I panic.'
I can fake it for a while, but then the truth comes and gets me.
—Sylvia

If you ever learned to drive, ride a bike, ski, or snowboard, you know you didn't feel safe until you learned how to stop. It's the same in swimming. You need to know how to stop in order to feel safe. Stop your arms and legs? No, stop yourself from panicking. Once you can remain stopped, you can learn the simple building blocks and mechanics of swimming.

CONTROL GIVES CONFIDENCE
CONFIDENCE ENABLES LEARNING

Overcoming fear *must* precede learning to swim. Otherwise, the feelings of ease and freedom you desire to play, rest, and swim in shallow and deep water are not possible.

It's more important to stay in the 1st Circle than to float or put your face in the water, stand up, or tread water. If you stay in the 1st Circle, you'll be in control of whether you inhale water or not, stay floating or stand up, stay speedy or slow down. Once you can remain in control, you can do whatever you want to do. Do you see the importance of being in the 1st Circle?

$2+2=4$

YOU MUST BE ABLE TO REMAIN IN THE 1ST CIRCLE
IN ORDER TO LEARN TO SWIM.

HOW TO STAY IN CONTROL

You can stay in control (in the 1st Circle) by *feeling*. *Everything*. That's right. Slow down and *feel* everything that's happening in the moment. Feel whatever is there. Feel your internal "speed," feel buoyancy, feel tension, feel your chair, feel the air temperature, feel how much air you have or don't have, feel your left knee. Just feel. If feeling all of that is too much, just feel one of them. You'll probably have to slow down to feel.

DON'T EVEN THINK ABOUT
SKIPPING THE STEP OF FEELING

To be in control, we have to feel. And because feeling happens in only one place—our bodies—when we focus on what we're feeling, we stay in our bodies. Where our focus is, we are. Feeling keeps us in our bodies and keeps us in control.

Often, we use thinking to negotiate an unfamiliar situation. But in some situations, such as overcoming your fear in water, thinking does not work best. It works better to feel. When we think too much, we lose touch with feelings.

If you let yourself feel, you'll get a sense of what to do next. Proceed slowly enough to keep feeling. Follow your internal "instructions." Give yourself permission (and get permission from anyone you're with) to slow down and feel. You need to stay slow. If you do this, you cannot help but succeed.

Please let yourself off the hook for not learning to swim if you tried before. You were probably not asked to go slowly and listen to your internal signals, feel them, and follow their instructions. But these were absolutely essential!

Have you watched a baby learn to walk? She didn't hurry herself. She had no deadline. She didn't try to run before she could walk. She didn't criticize herself as she learned. She didn't compare herself to the neighbor baby or compete. She was completely self-absorbed—that is, 100% in her body. She was in the 1st Circle. That's why a skill as intricate as walking takes only a few weeks for a baby to learn completely.

The baby is mindful—completely present. The 5 Circles ascending depict loss of control. The 5 Circles descending (pictured later in the book) depict gaining control. This definition of mindfulness will enable vast numbers of people to learn in areas where fear once stopped them.

STEP 3: PERMISSION TO GO AT YOUR OWN PACE

Where you are right now with your swimming is precisely the perfect place for you. Without effort, you'll find your way to your goals, and your goals will find their way to you. Gradually, as you spend time in the water and you open up to new thoughts and feelings, you move forward. Change happens, sometimes in the pool, sometimes between pool sessions, sometimes in your dreams.

You may have a sense of new information coming to you. Simply by picking up this book, something began to shift. An opening was created. Each conscious and unconscious moment that you're engaged in this book, you'll fill in a bit of space in this new opening. Trust that you're doing exactly what's appropriate for you just by being yourself. You'll reach your swimming goals simply by doing what's fun.

Let yourself move one easy step at a time. Be there for each step. Experience the water. Listen to your body: it will tell you what you need to know in the moment. When you're "home," i.e., in your body, you can hear what it tells you. You automatically translate that into security, action, floating, swimming. However if you're not home, you can't hear your body's instructions or take care of yourself well. When the time comes, if you're practicing a skill that doesn't seem to be working, stop and come back to your body. Better yet, don't practice a physical skill; practice only being in your body. Out of this, a physical skill will arise.

Only your body can tell you when it's time to do something new. You learn beautifully when you go at your own pace. In fact, nothing can prevent you from progressing all the way to your goals if you go at your own pace.

> *Your method has allowed me to go as slowly as I want, which I've never experienced before in learning a new sport. I'm really excited about swimming, being in water for the first time in my life and welcoming the whole new world that is opening up to me.*
>
> —Darlene

STEP 4: WHAT IS SAFETY?

As mentioned above, for the purposes of this course, safety is your ability to remain in control of yourself. Safety is also having choices about how to respond rather than responding automatically but inappropriately because of panic.

Yes, there's another kind of safety, too…the pool rules: "don't run on the deck, don't push, don't chew gum in the pool (to avoid choking), don't leave your child unattended at the pool." But your ability to remain in control of yourself in water is the key to enjoying every day at the pool, making intelligent choices, and coming through a common swimming misadventure unharmed.

What's a misadventure? It's accidentally bumping into someone in the water or getting a nose full of water or stepping into a hole at the lake. These things happen. Handling these events easily with no concern whatsoever is about knowing how the water works and remaining present.

**Handling surprises well:
staying in your body**

2+2=4

IF A PERSON REMAINS IN CONTROL, HE HAS A BETTER CHANCE OF REMAINING SAFE THAN IF HE LOSES CONTROL.

For example, if someone loses control, he may inhale while he's still under water. Or, he may thrash in just three feet of water, keeping himself below the surface instead of simply standing up. In both these situations, the person is "not there." He is out of his body. If he were present, he wouldn't do these things.

As we've said, the solution was always thought to be, "learn to swim," meaning "learn strokes." The solution is, actually, "learn to stay present." If you were present, you'd be able to feel the water holding you up. You'd notice that you still have enough air to stand up or get to the side. You'd be able to see how close to the surface you are or that you're at the surface already. If you weren't at the surface, you'd be able to take yourself there and get air even if you had never learned how to do it before.

If you were present, you'd be "notified" by your intuition what your next step is—guaranteed. When you need to know something and you're calm, your next step just comes to you. Have you found this to be true in other parts of your life? *This is how you learned to walk.*

How to Stay in Your Body

To stay in your body, feel. Go slowly. If you focus on your feeling, whatever the feeling is, whether easy or tense, warm or cold, happy or sad, your focus will be in your body. Since you can't be in two places at once, if you feel, you'll keep yourself in your body. You'll prevent yourself from panicking. You will be smack in the very place that healing takes place. *Herein lies one of the most powerful skills we can perform as humans: remaining in control—remaining in our bodies.* If you follow this book, you'll learn to prevent panic and stay in control. You'll learn it by overcoming your fear in water. The message is repeated often to help you develop this new habit in water.

Is It Easy to Remain Present?

Let's go back to the diagram of The 5 Circles of the spirit leaving the body.

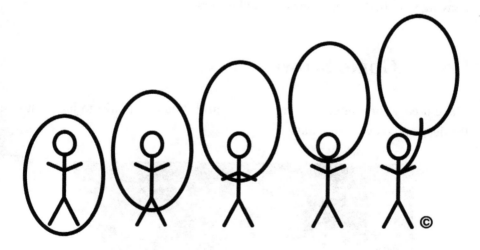

Review

Question: Why would we leave our bodies if it causes us to lose control?
Answer: We leave because we don't want to feel pain, physical or emotional.

But, we're not *in control of* avoiding the pain. We avoid it by habit:

Approaching pain → LEAVE

Approaching pain → LEAVE

Breaking this habit is a step toward more empowered living, and freedom in water. Slow down and feel. If you slow down early enough, pain (in the form of anxiety) will not be a factor. If you practice this in the pool, keeping yourself in your body will become a habit.

In extreme situations, it might be essential to call heavily on this new muscle, the muscle of being able to keep yourself in your body to remain in control. Hopefully, you'll never be in such a situation. But if you are, it can save your life.

To make it comfortable to stay present if you begin to feel afraid, slow down and stop. Feel just a "teaspoon" at a time.

Leaving your body (panicking) would be worse.

STEP 5: GOING SLOWLY

Make it easy for yourself to remain in control. You don't have to jump into the deep end on your first day.

If you start slowly and do whatever allows you to remain in control at all times, you'll overcome your fear. You'll come to situations that used to make you afraid, and you'll be able to handle them with new ease. For now, take them very slowly. You may have to stay in one place for a while. This is the natural process of healing and learning. Go slowly enough that you don't mind feeling your feelings. Sometimes it requires time, writing, talking, and feeling things you hadn't planned to feel. Give thanks. It's part of the process of becoming more yourself and free in water. The process looks different for each person, and each person's process is right.

STEP 6: STAY TRUE TO YOURSELF

It can be said that the 1st Circle is a picture of what it looks like to stay true to yourself. In the 1st Circle, you and your body are in the same place; you're "in true."

Being "in true" is a term used about bicycle wheels and spokes when they are in perfect alignment. Stay in true, yourself.

Staying true to yourself—
staying in your body

Each time you make a decision that allows you to stay true to yourself, you build self-trust. You are building a stronger foundation of self-trust in the water. It's your confidence infrastructure.

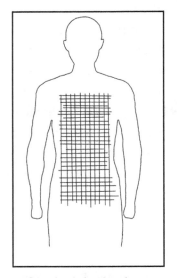

Light Infrastructure: Relatively
few choices made to stay
true to yourself. Relatively
little confidence.

Greater Infrastructure:
Many choices made
to stay true to yourself.
Relatively high confidence.

If you want to do X, do it. If you don't want to do X, don't do it. If not doing X makes you feel worse, then you actually do want to do it. Doing it will build self-trust.

If, in the water, you're curious about something and you feel safe exploring it, stay true to yourself and explore it. Not doing so could be disappointing.

If you want to explore something in the water and you don't feel safe, then, to stay true to yourself—to stay in the 1st Circle—you may need to ask for help or make it feel safe in another way.

2+2=4
WHATEVER IT TAKES FOR YOU TO STAY TRUE
TO YOURSELF IS WORTH DOING.

Learning will succeed if you stay true to yourself. If you don't, you'll delay or prevent learning.

STEP 7: HAVE FUN

Where you are when you're having fun

TWO KINDS OF FUN

What are your beliefs about having fun in water?
Do you believe you can have fun doing things in any part of the pool? Is this hard to believe?

Learning can be fun, as you know. Can it can be fun to learn to swim? This book is written to make each step small enough that nothing is scary, you understand everything you're doing, and you're game for each new experience. People tell me that each new experience is fun. If it's *not* fun, stop. Find another way. Ask yourself what you would enjoy doing that's in between where you are and where you want to be.

Tiny steps are safest for keeping things fun.

Having fun is a most natural state for you. A willingness to go slowly and stay comfortable will pave your way to a good experience. Are you willing to take the time?

There are two kinds of fun. We often think of fun as the way we feel when we're doubled over, slapping our knees laughing. That's one kind of fun.

In other kind of fun, you're not necessarily doubled over laughing, but if someone were to ask you if you wanted to stop, you'd say no. You're having a different kind of fun: exploring, satisfying your curiosity, absorbing information, finding a new path.

Everything in this book—every step—is designed to be fun. We learn so naturally and easily when we have fun. We don't use effort, yet we learn anyway.

If something stops being fun as you practice the teachings of this book, stop. Change the subject. Being unhappy is not a good use of your time...unless you're having fun being unhappy. (Don't laugh. I've seen it, and you probably have, too.)

IF IT'S NOT FUN, DON'T DO IT

You may say, "Sometimes if I push myself, I have a breakthrough." Outside the pool, this is common. If you pulled all-nighters as a student in order to turn in a paper in the morning, pushing helped. If you're an athlete and you push yourself during competition in order to do better, pushing makes a difference. In the pool, if it's *fun* to push, go ahead. If it's *not* fun, stop.

2+2=4

IF YOU'RE NOT HAVING FUN, YOU'RE NOT IN THE 1ST CIRCLE.
IT'S ESSENTIAL TO HAVE FUN.

When you're overcoming fear, any "breakthroughs" that are accomplished by pushing will not stick. Pushing yourself to perform a skill so that you can check it off your list is an empty victory. And, it's not stable. Many swimming students have been told by their instructors, "There! You've got it. Now you just need to practice." But the students knew in their bones that they didn't have it, even if it looked as if they did.

The most important reason to avoid pushing is that it's scary; it takes you out of the 1st Circle. We have established (well, I have…have you?) that it's our #1 priority to practice being in the 1st Circle all the time: practice comfort and control to become expert at comfort and control. You don't need to be better at scaring yourself, so don't practice anything that puts you in the 2nd Circle or higher.

If you feel even a hint of frustration, back up, regroup and start again. Frustration is the 3rd Circle. Regrouping looks like this:

It fell apart.   I regrouped.

If there's another hint of frustration, stop and change the subject. You don't have to have a crummy time learning to swim. It can all be fun. If it's not one kind of fun or the other, you're pushing. Come back to the 1st Circle where you can enjoy yourself.

PUSHING HINDERS LEARNING

STEP 8: YOUR GOALS AND WILDEST DREAMS

Identifying your goals and wildest dreams for swimming expands your thinking. Write down your goals for learning to swim:

1. _____
2. _____
3. _____
4. _____

Is comfort your Number 1 goal? I hope so, but I'm not allowed to vote. Now write down your wildest dreams for swimming. Be outrageous. No holds barred!

1. _____

2. _____

3. _____

4. _____

When you identify and write down your goals, you establish a direction for yourself. It's more powerful to state them in words, spoken or written, than simply to think about them. By writing down your goals and wildest dreams, you add weight to them. You anchor them in your infrastructure. If you tell someone your goals, someone you trust, you anchor them still deeper.

If you were to show someone where your goals were relative to your arms' reach, where would they be?

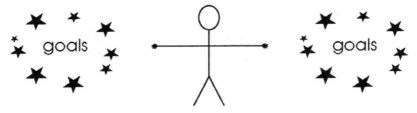

Your goals are just outside your present reach.
It requires stretching or growth to reach them.

They would probably be just beyond your present reach. Accomplishing them requires stretching or growth.

Now, relative to your arms' reach, where would your wildest dreams be?

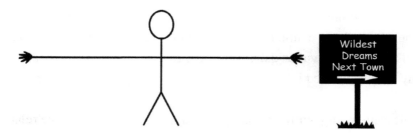

Your wildest dreams are well beyond your present reach, but since they reach further, *you* reach further. You grow. This wide expanse is your mental space "assigned" to reaching your swimming dreams. You may have heard the phrase, "space abhors a vacuum." The larger the empty space, the more information you'll naturally pull in to fill it. This requires no effort.

STEP 9: YOUR RELATIONSHIP TO YOUR GOALS

Here you sit in your chair. Nearby are the goals you want to reach. What's between you and your goals? How do you feel about them? Will you need to conquer them? Cajole them? Chase them? Trick them? Work hard? Push yourself? Grow?

Would it work to be gracious with them? To give them room?

Often, we think of our goals—especially if they've been elusive—as something we have to bear down upon and work hard to reach. We brace ourselves for the big push. If you feel this way about your swimming goals, will it help you get started? Not likely.

Between you and your goals are your feelings about them—and also the steps required to reach them. Let's talk about feelings.

If there were a new person with whom you wanted to have dinner, and you did all the work of arranging the details—calling him/her, making reservations at a restaurant and time of his/her choice, picking him/her up, taking him/her home—and you continued to try to build a friendship by handling all the details yourself date after date, would the relationship work? Probably not. Many of us have tried it.

It's the same with your relationship to your goals. Your part of the relationship is to do what's fun and comfortable—what you feel good about. The rest is out of your hands.

At times you may be afraid that you won't reach the goal. You may think you're doing something wrong and try to figure it out. This causes you to go into your head and disconnect from your body's knowing and the hope and the optimism you started with. The truth is, nothing's wrong: it's inevitable that you'll reach your swimming goal if you're willing to do what's fun and let it come at its own pace.

What if you treated your goals with respect? Gave them room? Didn't crowd them, chase them, or threaten them? When you insist that they hurry, they retreat. When you're willing to give them all the time they need and you enjoy the ride, they come as soon as possible.

You may say again, "But many times I reach my goals by pushing." True. And there are times when pushing is appropriate. The process of learning to overcome fear, however, is not one of those times. Try *not* pushing yourself and see how it works. You'll find that not only is it healing, but you'll enjoy yourself in water perhaps for the first time. You'll build a new you in the water. You'll get there by trusting your feelings, your body, your intuition.

YOU	GOAL	YOU	GOAL →

You have fun and let the goal
come to you. This is easy.

You push. It becomes frustrating.
Progress is prevented or delayed.

STEP 10: IMPACT AND BENEFITS OF BEING AFRAID IN WATER

List the ways that your life has been impacted by being afraid in water:

1. _____
2. _____
3. _____
4. _____

Now answer this question: How has my fear in water served me in my life? What has been *good* about it?

Sometimes people think this is a trick question. It's not meant to be. There are *benefits* you have derived (fairly, innocently) from being afraid in water. How has it come in handy for you? List the ways here:

1. _____
2. _____
3. _____

To help you remember the benefits, note some that other people have listed:

_____ I didn't have to worry about being seen in a bathing suit.

_____ It allowed me to stay safe rather than taking risks.

_____ I didn't have to worry about ruining my hair.

_____ I didn't have to be vulnerable or look as though I didn't know what I was doing.

_____ I didn't have to worry about my makeup.

_____ I received attention from my family and friends.

_____ I had more time for myself.

_____ It brought me closer to another family member who also couldn't swim.

_____ It allowed me to become closer to a group of people for whom it was "hip" to not swim.

_____ It kept me alive because I stayed away from dangerous situations.

_____ I have a great story about why I don't swim.

_____ I saved money on bathing suits since mine never wore out.

_____ I got many parent/family points for playing with the kids instead of going to a swimming social function.

_____ There were no benefits whatsoever. I was always missing the fun. I was embarrassed that I couldn't participate.

Be as honest as you can be with yourself. If there's something you don't accept in yourself, it can be more difficult to be honest about it. You can only be as honest as you are self-accepting.

Honesty gets you to your goal most quickly. You're the only person who sees your answers. Your answers are okay, whatever they are. As an instructor of this teaching, I have heard just about *everything*, and I never heard a response that was not understandable. It's okay to have the beliefs you have, even if they sound silly to you.

Now that you've begun the process of overcoming your fear, you've indirectly said, "By undertaking this learning, I am giving up the benefits I once derived from being afraid in water." Ask yourself, "Am I ready to be finished with these benefits?" If you're ready to be finished with them, fine.

If not, that's fine, too.

It's helpful just to know the truth. If you're not finished with one or more of them, it's completely okay. Don't push yourself to be done with them. Let yourself be where you are. In some way they make you feel safe. They are healing you.

By identifying the benefits of being afraid in water, you have now given yourself a choice. Having a choice is a great place to be.

HAVING A CHOICE MEANS YOU'RE IN CONTROL

It doesn't matter *what* you choose; it just matters that you have a choice. You could choose to accept the benefits you derive from being afraid and let them be there. They are okay. Or, you could decide to give up the benefits because you're finished with them. *One choice is not better or more advanced than another.* The goal is to be true to yourself. If you cannot accept that you're where you are with regard to your beliefs, perhaps you can accept that you cannot accept it. *That's good enough.*

STEP 11: UNDERSTANDING SELF-CONSCIOUSNESS

If you anticipate that you might feel self-conscious at the pool, ask yourself where "you" are. Are you over in someone else's eyes looking back at yourself. That's a good example of being out of your body. If you come back "home," you can do what's best for you.

Chances are that if someone's watching you, they're *interested* in what you're doing, not critical. Then they lose interest. There's a chance that they're on the deck because they cannot yet do what you're learning to do. Why are most of the adults on the deck, in chairs? Maybe they don't want to get wet, or maybe they're afraid. Why are adults vertical in the shallow end, not swimming? Could some of them be afraid, too?

If you feel self-conscious, remember this: you're there for yourself only, and only you can give this to yourself. You have your best chance of success if you keep your focus on yourself and honor the *feeling in your body*. This is practicing staying in your body. And this practice will take you where you want to go in swimming.

STEP 12: WARM UP TO GETTING IN

You may now be ready to think about getting into the water. If you understand what I've said so far, we're on the same page. Are you ready to find a pool? To get in? What do you feel when you think about it? Excitement? Fear? Nervousness? If it doesn't feel like fun to think about it, then what would make it fun? Going with a friend? Not pushing yourself? Being in a class? Being near a lifeguard? Being warm? Being in a pool with no deep end? Having no splashing kids around? Not going at all? All of these are okay.

One reason for using warm pools is that fear, itself, is cold. Generally someone who is afraid in water is colder in the pool than someone who is not afraid.

WHY POOLS (AND YOU) SHOULD BE WARM FOR LEARNING

An ideal water temperature for learning is 92° to 95° F (33° C). That's hot for air, but not for water. Warmth makes all the difference in your ability to enjoy yourself and stay present.

When you're warm, you can focus on your practice. In school, would you have been expected to learn in classrooms that were 40 degrees? Likewise, learning pools should be warm. In the early stages of learning, there's not a lot of activity. You need to be warm without exercising. In our classes we are in the water for two hours at a time. This allows us to relax and go slowly. Students are very happy with the warm water and the time we have in the pool.

If you can't find a warm pool, I suggest purchasing a one- or two-millimeter wetsuit (neoprene) shirt. A thin wetsuit like this should do the trick. It adds a bit of buoyancy, but it won't hurt your learning at all. It's tremendously worthwhile.

When trying on and purchasing a wetsuit shirt, make sure it has zero gaps and zero wrinkles. If it's not snug, it won't keep you warm.

STEP 13: SET YOURSELF UP TO SUCCEED

Create the situation you need in order to be comfortable. What would a fun, successful visit to the pool be like? Set up your visit so that you can enjoy yourself. Write it here:

1. _____

2. _____

3. _____

FINDING THE RIGHT POOL

To maximize your chances of success, look for the right pool. Ideally it will be:

1. Warm (92° to 95° F – 33° C)

2. In a convenient location

3. Available at hours that work for you

4. Clean

For a list of pools in your area, go to www.swimmersguide.com. Most heated swimming pools are kept at temperatures between 80° and 84°. Some are kept between 85° and 90°. Pools in the low- to mid-80s feel chilly to most new swimmers. Typically you can find warm water at centers for people with disabilities, at Easter Seals organizations, or hospital therapy pools. There are also warm pools in hot springs locations (where we teach some of our classes). Some of the cities where there are centers for people with disabilities are San Francisco (the Janet Pomeroy Center) and Minneapolis (the Courage Center). Some hotels have warm pools and allow community swimming. Call around.

At centers for people with disabilities, you may need a prescription to use the pool for their insurance purposes. These prescriptions can be acquired from doctors or health care practitioners. If you're self-conscious about asking for this prescription, take note: are you outside of your body? If so, bring yourself back and do what's best for you.

Try not to compromise. To compromise in this case may not be staying true to yourself. Go to this pool. Observe the setting. What's going on? Will you be able to feel in control there if you follow your plan?

STEP 14: STARTING FROM CALM

When you're learning something new, you'll be most comfortable if you let yourself be where you are.

If you're not calm, stop and feel your discomfort. Don't try to make it disappear. Bring your attention, your self, all the way into your body. What does your body need in order to be comfortable? Give it to yourself, whatever it is. Don't proceed until you're comfortable.

It doesn't matter *what* you do to be calm. It only matters that you feel calm and in control. This can't be emphasized enough. Keeping yourself comfortable is the whole point. If you're enjoying yourself, you'll want to continue.

Your new connection with water automatically emerges when you're in your body, listening to it, and letting yourself feel. Give yourself time to come home. From here, new ideas and information come to you.

Simply by being committed to your swimming and following the steps in this book—or even reading them—you've accelerated the learning/healing process.

STEP 15: BEING IN YOUR BODY VS. BEING IN YOUR HEAD

Here is an exercise that someone could read to you slowly as you listen. Or, you can record it on your phone and play it back:

Close your eyes. Think about your breakfast this morning. Did you have breakfast? Did you have your favorite breakfast? Did you go out for breakfast? Did you eat alone?

Now feel your feet. Feel your feet inside your shoes. Feel their temperature. Are they warm enough? Are they comfortable? Do they feel squeezed?

Now think about breakfast again. What did you have? Did you read as you ate? Did you take your time? Did you hurry?

Now feel your feet again. What position are they in? Are they moving? How are your toes? Now think about breakfast again. Did you eat enough?

Notice how your location changes as you go from breakfast to feet. When you think about breakfast, your location is in your head. When you feel your feet, your location is in your feet. Head. Feet. Head. Feet.

It's useful to know how *feeling* and thinking change the location of your awareness, the location of you. By feeling, you tune into your body and yourself.

Today or soon, go back to this place you've found to go swimming and get into the water. Take the easy route.

Here's a diagram of you on the easy route.

Once you're in the water, just stand there. Absorb the surroundings. Hold onto the wall. Lean against it and breathe. You're in the water. You're on a new path. Stay as long as you're enjoying yourself. There's nothing else to do for now.

**Have fun learning. This is the "WahWah Sisterhood,"
Orlando Beginning class, 2004.**

CONTRACT WITH YOURSELF

I _____ have decided once and for
all that I want to overcome my fear of being in water (shallow or
deep) and to learn to swim the way I've always dreamt I could.
I agree to give myself the best possible chance of learning. This
means I will (check all that you agree to):

_____ give myself all the time it takes

_____ allow myself to stay safe all the time

_____ allow myself to have fun all the time

_____ stay comfortable

_____ learn what it feels like to stay in my body

_____ learn how to bring myself back into my body

_____ allow myself to leave the pool while I am still happy

_____ check my beliefs from time to time to measure my progress

_____ be honest with myself

_____ be gentle with myself

_____ examine—if the opportunity arises—any lack of gentleness,
and review the section about it in this book (Steps 51 and 53)

_____ know that if I do these things, I can only succeed in reaching
my goals.

Signed, _____

Dated _____

Any lingering thoughts? List them:

1. _____

2. _____

STEP 16: GET THE BIG PICTURE

When you decide to learn to swim and you do something about it, you have a natural propensity to pay attention, follow directions, and try to do things correctly so that it will work. You want to "get it," and you're prepared to work for it.

Rest easy. You'll get it. It's not that you'll get it if you do everything "perfectly." It's not that you'll get it if you push hard enough. It's simply that when you let yourself have fun and proceed at a comfortable pace, staying in one place for a while, then magically moving forward as more learning takes place, you naturally come upon "it." "It" is total control in the water.

I can't imagine why this isn't the universal way swimming is taught.
—Margaret

You become comfortable in water, shallow and deep, and begin to swim without effort. *It's inevitable.*

You'll learn some of what you're seeking by reading these steps. But you have to *feel* the steps of learning in the water to get to know it.

Please let it happen. Tell yourself, "I don't have to push myself. Swimming will come to me naturally if I just take it easy and have fun." If something is uncomfortable, don't put up with it. You must have skipped a step. Stop and go back to what's comfortable. Comfort and fun are your shortcuts to success.

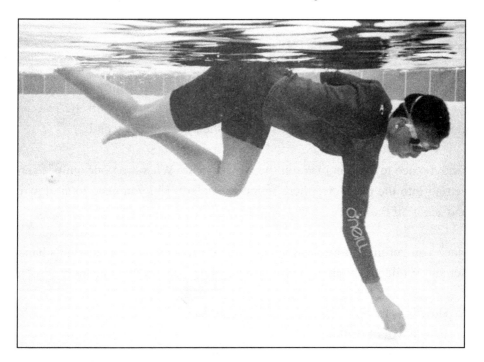

STUDENTS' BILL OF RIGHTS

In all classes, we hold these student rights to be self-evident.

1. The right to feel safe.
2. The right to be comfortable.
3. The right to ask all your questions.
4. The right to receive correct answers.
5. The right to learn at your own pace.
6. The right to be taught by a qualified, knowledgeable instructor.
7. The right to embody Step 1 before being presented with Step 2.
8. The right to be supported.
9. The right to share your experience with someone.
10. The right to say no.

Step 17: Getting in

You've considered what you need to do in order to make your first foray into the pool. You've given yourself permission to stay true to yourself. You've gone to the pool of your choice. You're at the pool's shallow end.

Find a place to stop and take in the whole scene. What are your options for getting into the pool? Are there stairs? A ladder? Will you need to sit down and scoot off the edge?

Once you get in, you might just lean against the wall and watch what's happening. While you're there, notice your feelings and let them be there.

How is your heart rate? Normal or elevated?
How is your breathing?
How is your "speed," that is, your internal vibration?
Do you feel tense or calm?
How is your balance?
How would you feel if you were away from the wall?

All these measures in your body are signals. You wouldn't want to ignore or override them. You'd want to be aware of them and let them be there. They are all okay. If something is uncomfortable, move to make yourself comfortable. Only then will you have attention to spare for learning.

Do this every time you get into the pool as a way to establish a safe and comfortable beginning as a habit.

PRESSURE ON YOUR CHEST

Sometimes people feel pressure on their chest when they get into the water and submerge up to their shoulders. This is normal. If you don't feel it, that's fine. But if you do, it may feel as though your breathing is constricted. Stand up straighter or go to shallower water to relieve this feeling, for now.

When you are in water, it exerts pressure on your body. You probably don't feel it anywhere except your chest. You feel it there because the air in your chest is less dense than water. You don't feel pressure on other parts of your body because the density of the rest of your body is closer to that of water.

Don't force yourself to be comfortable with this pressure on your chest. Proceed at your own pace. Stay happy. If it sounds like fun, drop down so that your chest is under water again, feel the pressure *and your resistance to it*: then come back up before it gets uncomfortable. Feel it, allow yourself to resist it, and then come up. Rest. Do it again, if you're willing. Do it as long as you enjoy it. If this is what you learn today in the pool, it's enough.

STEP 18: LETTER TO THE WATER

Here's a rich exercise. To some people, the benefits of writing a letter to the water are obvious. Others think I'm nuts. Or they hope no one sees them. I ask you to surrender and just do it. It'll help you. It's just for you.

Grab a sheet of paper and write to the water as though it were a person. Write your feelings. Write your thoughts, positive or negative, about shallow water, deep water, the drain, whatever. Write until you can write no more. Dump all your feelings out on the page. You're walking around in the world with a lot of feelings, many negative, about the water. You don't need to carry these around. To write them down helps you to heal. The more you write, the less you'll carry afterward. Write it all. Take your time.

One of my students, a self-described macho retired Oakland, California police officer, wrote ten pages for his conversation with the water. Later he became one of our beloved instructors.

Here are two sample letters from past students.

SAMPLE 1 FROM DEBORAH:

Hello, Water,

It's me. You know I'm scared. You have never been a friend to me. You have taken me to the depths of darkness. You at the same time have shown me some really beautiful things. I've enjoyed your warmth and at the same time I was scared that you'd take it away. You've made me feel conflicting feelings such as happiness and fear. I've missed so many opportunities and joys because I am afraid of you.

Today I am taking control of my life. I am still afraid, but I am going to take control.

I will not let anyone push me anymore.

I will not leave my body to your satisfaction.

I will remain in control in the here and now.

I will master my feelings.

My Emotions Come From The Following Experiences:

1. Kyra trying to teach me to swim in a public pool. I felt uncomfortable because I didn't look good in my swimsuit, because too many people were in the pool, because the pool had urine in it, because people would laugh when they realized I couldn't swim. Because I stepped on glass and cut my foot. I was more afraid when I left the pool than before I got in.

2. Pepperdine University: Peter pushes me in the pool's deep end. I stay under until Mark pulls me out. I was so grateful I married him.

3. Swimming lessons with my six-year-old son. He learns, I get a staph infection.

4. Rafting in Sacramento. I get knocked out of the raft by a stranger. My boyfriend fishes me out. You guessed it. I married him, too.

5. Rafting in Brazil. Rafting was great. Then the tour guide got this brilliant idea to have everyone get out of the rafts and slide down the natural waterfall and go through a few rapids. It took me 30 minutes to realize I lost one of my contacts under the water. Now that I understand "leaving my body" I can tell you that I left my body the minute my feet were knocked from under me. I lost control. I didn't enjoy any of these incidents with water. They all caused pain and fear just when I thought I'd have some fun.

6. My sixth experience was the Miracle Swimming introductory class I took in Berkeley. I was so scared I was 20 minutes late. I just stood outside the class trying to get the nerve to knock on the door. Finally, a kid came by and said, "Lady, they're in there. I'll knock for you." He began to kick the door. It was opened by a black man. I was shocked he was my new instructor. Being African American, [I am, too], he was the last person I expected to see.

7. This was the beginning of my journey of learning to conquer my fear of water. You see, before I went near the water again, I needed to admit I was scared. I readily admitted this when I read the course description for this class. It was exciting yet scary. I met a friend at the class, another African American woman whom I had worked with in the past. We bonded. We enjoyed the class. Our instructor understood we were afraid. He talked to us for hours. He addressed all our fears. We felt comfortable and most of all, capable. When he finished talking and asked us to get in the pool, we were all raring to go. This was my best experience ever in the water. Why? Because I was not pushed, cut, hurt, shoved, or sick. Because it was warm, I was safe, I was in control. At the end of class I begged to stay. I was having fun.

Hello, Deb,

It's me, Water. I am not the enemy. I am not scary. I am just like air: I exist. You need me to live. I am not the cause of your bad experiences; look at your notes. I only exist to keep you alive. If you open up you'll see that I am not scary; I am nourishing, cleansing, enjoyable, and good. If you weren't afraid you'd see that I am fun. That you need and like me. That together we could do all kinds of things. That if you trust me you cannot be hurt by me. That others caused your fear. I just am.

SAMPLE 2 FROM WILL:

Dear Water,

I have feared and hated you much of my life as if you were to blame. I was convinced that if I gave myself to you, you'd be intent on doing me harm. Perhaps in a past life I drowned and have carried that memory locked deep inside me. So, I turned away from you, put you out of my mind, and concerned myself with other pursuits. Perhaps fearing, hating, and ignoring you all this time has served some purpose, but I am at a loss to define it. Now, in calm and perhaps with greater wisdom, I see that I've cut myself off from half of the world's mysteries and wonders to see. I've begun visiting wonderful and mystical areas on land, but what of all that you have to offer? It calls to me, but as yet, I lack the confidence to pursue it. I realize now that you offer neither fear nor love. You just are, and my perception of you is my own creation. I have the power to change that perception by understanding more of myself and how I am when we are together. Perhaps you're just so vast that you care not whether I fear or love you. That, perhaps, I am insignificant in your eyes. That you could cause me to not trust you, but once again that would be of my own creation.

Yesterday, I found out that you would hold me up, something I never expected. Were you being benevolent? It would be nice to think so, but I am beginning to realize that just as you're in me with no intention, so am

I naturally in you. Whether I float or not, or how well, is simply what's true for me. How I choose to accept and use that truth is up to me. And there's more to learn. So, whether you care or not, I offer my apology to you for the way I felt. You did nothing, and my experience has always been just my feelings and understanding of me, and me alone when I am around you.

Dear Will,

Apology accepted. But you're wrong about me. You believe I don't care, but the truth is, I care much. I call to all with a simple message, "Come, enjoy all the wonders and mysteries I enfold." It's true that relative to your physical existence, I am vast. You perhaps, at one time, saw tremendous power for harm in that expanse. And sometimes, terrible things happen, although not of my own intention. As you're a slave to your own feelings and beliefs, I too am a slave to the rotation of the Earth and Moon, the winds, and the role I must play. I have neither the power to deliberately harm nor to help; therefore, I must entrust you to yourselves and your own strengths and weaknesses. But that never, in any way, diminishes my wishes for you in feeling comfortable with me. I look forward to seeing you soon.

Now it's your turn. What would you say to the water? Stop reading, get a sheet of paper, and do this exercise. A few blank lines are given below to jot your first thoughts in case you want to do this later. You don't want to miss this.

My Letter to Water

_____

_____

Then, when you've said it all, ask the water if it has a reply. No kidding. What would the water say to you? Give it a try. It's for you alone. You might learn something.

STEP 19: MIAMI TO SEATTLE

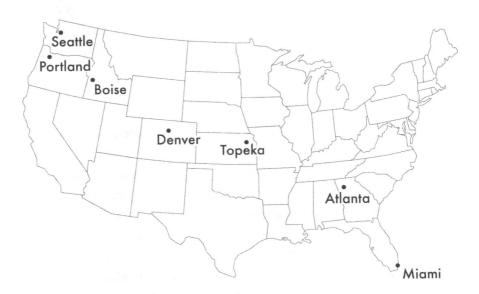

If you wanted to walk from Miami to Seattle, you could. Sure, it would take a while. Sure, you would need support. But if you had enough time, food, rest, shelter, and warmth, and you wanted to do it, you could. The journey from where you are now with your swimming to where you want to be is similar to a walk from Miami to Seattle. It might seem just as far, but it won't be. Just as that walk can be made wonderful and thoroughly enjoyable, so can the path to your complete freedom and competence in water. If you take one step at a time and stay comfortable, it's inevitable that you'll get there.

If, on your walk from Miami to Seattle, you tried to leave Topeka to go to Denver before you had gone from Miami to Atlanta, it wouldn't work. It simply cannot be done. In the same way, it's not possible to, say, learn to tread water comfortably in the deep before you learn to be comfortable in the deep. And you cannot expect to learn freestyle and breathing before you're at ease in water in general.

To try to do either of these is to skip a boatload of steps. I have observed that:

THE ONLY CAUSE OF PROBLEMS IS SKIPPING STEPS

Please check the truth of that statement for yourself.

No wonder swimming lessons didn't meet your expectations. You were trying to leave Boise while you were still in Miami.

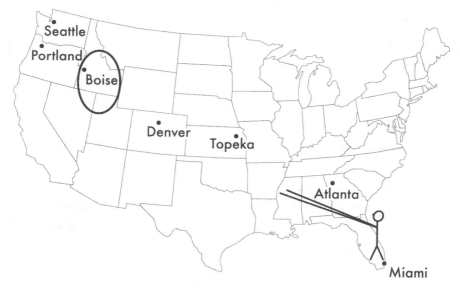

Body in Miami, attention in Boise

However, if you start at Step 1 and master it before going to Step 2, and you master Step 2 before going to Step 3 and continue this way, you can't possibly fail to reach your goals. This is the way I hope you'll proceed. Furthermore, Step 1 and Step 2 are not physical skills. They are the steps of understanding and presence.

Step 20: Checking Things Off the List vs. Learning Them

Which would you rather do? Learn and "own" the skill of floating, or float once, show an instructor, have her check you off a list as having floated, and try to learn the next, more advanced skill?

> *Learning means gaining a permanent new understanding of, and ease with, a skill or idea. We're not interested in temporary gains. Learning happens when you're present to a new skill and you let yourself embody it. The skill then becomes a part of you. If you do it enough, it will become part of you for life.*

If you passed a swimming test to graduate from high school or college by being checked off the list for performing a task once—gritting your teeth, hanging on by your fingernails, holding your breath to the bursting point, and living till the end of it—did you really "pass" the swimming test?

Surely you asked yourself, "What good is this?"

Many steps were skipped between where you were when you began your swimming and where you were said to be when you "passed" the swimming test. More steps were skipped between your swimming test and receiving carte blanche to graduate as "safe in the water." Obviously, you were not safe in the water.

Many schools have dropped the swimming requirement to graduate. I believe that the elimination of this requirement was due to the lack of a successful swimming program for afraid students. Passing a swimming test was a well-intentioned idea, but for students who failed the test, there had to be a program in place for them to be successful. Sadly, it usually wasn't. It looked silly to have a requirement and no way for afraid students to meet it. Therefore, it was dropped, and students didn't receive the intended benefit. Now that there's a proven path to success, the requirement could be reinstated so that all can become safe in water.

Jeannie

When you look at Jeannie, would you say that she's calm? Where is she? She's "home." This is a photo of her in an advanced class she took with us in the ocean. Jeannie wasn't always this way. In fact, she quit high school to dodge the swimming requirement for graduation! Now she's one of our instructors.

Countless students have told us how they fudged passing their swimming requirement to graduate. One man went to the back of the line and kept going to the back until class was over. His instructor forgot to test him in the next class. A book could be filled with stories like these.

I presume that you would rather have taken a class that taught you how to be in control in water. *Then* you would have liked to learn how to swim. It turns out that overcoming fear of deep water IS learning to swim! As you experiment with this or that skill in the water, give yourself time to get to know it. Each is rich. Doing them will teach you more than just a new physical skill.

It will teach you about water. There's so much to absorb that's new. What's more, you can't do the same things on land.

"I'm Too Advanced for This"

Some will say, "I can already do this. Show me the bigger stuff." Many will say, "I am fine in shallow water. I love the water. It's the deep water that I'm afraid of. Show me what to do in the deep."

It so happens that if you really knew yourself in shallow water and you really knew how shallow water worked, you would be eager to try things in deep water. If you're not eager to get into deep water, you need to learn what you don't know about *water.* That is, find out how the water and your body work together in the shallow. And, learn how to stay in your body.

This will allow you to be in control in any situation in shallow water. When you become confident in shallow water, your learner's mind will impishly suggest that you try the same things in deep water. And if you have truly mastered shallow water, you'll have no problem doing these things in deep water.

If you have tried any of the exercises in this book before and they haven't "worked," I suggest that what was missing was your presence. The goal now is to do each of the steps with your complete presence of mind. When you have done this, you'll be in control of your little toe, your breath, your nose, and your balance, in any position in the shallow water. When you've done it enough, you won't wonder; you'll know.

As you read through the following exercises, take time to practice each one. If something seems too elementary, read the steps to make sure you haven't missed anything. When you're certain that you own a step on a certain front and there's no possible learning left for you in it, go on to the next one. Go slowly. If there truly is no more to learn about it, you will probably come upon your next step naturally.

Step 21: Your Beliefs About Water

Put a check mark next to the beliefs you hold. Check your gut-level beliefs, not your intellectual beliefs. Imagine that you're in the water as you consider each one.

_____ If I put my face in water, I'll get water in my nose or mouth.

_____ It's dangerous when I get water in my nose or mouth.

_____ If I get water in my nose or mouth, I'll struggle, sputter, cough, and possibly drown.

_____ If water gets into my mouth, I'll swallow it.

_____ If I relax in water, I'll drop straight to the bottom like a stone.

_____ Sometimes I can't keep my presence of mind in deep water.

_____ I am not a floater.

_____ I know I can float.

_____ I am not a swimmer yet.

_____ I was born a swimmer.

_____ It would be unwise of me to relax in water.

_____ I have to push myself in order to learn to swim.

_____ If I relax in water, I might lose control.

_____ I may not have adequate lung capacity to swim.

_____ Deep water works differently than shallow water.

_____ My mind works differently in deep water than it does in shallow water.

_____ It would be unwise of me to relax in deep water.

_____ If I relax in deep water, something dreadful will happen.

_____ Each breath I take must be maximal in case I don't get another one.

_____ I can't control my body well in shallow water.

_____ I can't control my body well in deep water.

_____ A skill that works in the shallow end won't necessarily work in the deep end.

_____ If I want to learn to swim, I have to follow the swimming instructor's directions, even if I don't want to.

_____ To float correctly, my body should be horizontal.

_____ Being able to float depends on where the bottom is.

_____ Being able to do other skills depends on where the bottom is.

_____ A person can't get air if s/he's in deep water because there's no bottom to stand on.

_____ When I'm in deep water, I must move vigorously to stay afloat.

_____ In deep water, I need skills that I don't need in shallow water.

_____ In order to rest, I need the bottom or the side.

_____ It's harder to breathe in deep water than in shallow water.

_____ Shallow water is as dangerous as deep water.

_____ Shallow water won't hold me up.

_____ Deep water won't hold me up.

_____ The water is more powerful than I am.

_____ I need to be more physically fit than I am to learn to swim.

_____ The method in this book may work for others, but it may not work for me.

_____ I don't trust myself in deep water.

Do You Have Other Beliefs About Yourself and the Water?

List them here:

_____

_____

Given that you have these beliefs, what would you expect your experience in the water to be like?

_____

_____

Would you feel free in deep water? No. And if you keep these beliefs, do you think you'll learn to be confident and free in water? No.

Your beliefs and feelings are okay, no matter what they are. You have to start somewhere. If you try to start from where you wish you were or where you think you should be, which is ahead of where you actually are, you'll skip steps. The way you're "supposed" to feel is the way you will feel once you allow yourself to feel the way you do feel.

You've come to this book to learn how to have the beliefs you want. True? You want to believe that water holds you up, that you can be at ease without worry, that you can remain in control, that swimming is fun even in deep water. You want to feel that you can enjoy being in a pool, a lake, on a raft, in the ocean, on and off a boat.

> *Alice laughed. "There's no use trying," she said.*
> *"One can't believe impossible things."*
> *"I dare say you haven't had much practice," said the Queen.*
> *"When I was your age I always did it for half an hour a day.*
> *Why, sometimes, I've believed as many as six impossible things*
> *before breakfast."*
>
> —*Through the Looking Glass,* Lewis Carroll

In order to *have* the experiences you want, you need to be able to *do* things differently. In order to be able to do those things differently (for example, the way you lie on the water, or put your face in it, or move through it) you need to *believe* differently. You therefore want to change your beliefs. Do you agree? You want to change the way you're *being* about the water or deep water.

STEP 22: BEING/DOING/HAVING

At the core of you is you, a spirit. This is pure goodness, light, peace, wisdom, and knowledge. This is my belief. Is it yours? It helps explain my entire thesis, all of my work. It is demonstrated by 100% of my students.

Just outside the core of you, are your beliefs. It's your beliefs that determine how you will "be" in the world. Your beliefs come from what you're taught by others or from your interpretation of your experiences. Your beliefs about your safety cause you to be either at ease in the water or tense in the water.

If your beliefs about being in deep water are scary, you'll be scared in the water. When you believe that water holds you up, or that you can remain in control in deep water, you'll no longer be afraid.

Just beyond your beliefs are the things you *do*. Your actions come from your beliefs. What have your beliefs led you to do?

For example, if you believe that water does not hold you up, then you won't want to let go of the wall. Or, if you believe you're supposed to be horizontal to float, you may struggle to keep your feet off the bottom.

If you believe that water holds you up, you'll let your hands and feet go where they naturally go when gravity and buoyancy have their say.

From the things you *believe* come the things you *do*. From the things you *do* come the experiences you *have*. Therefore, what you *believe* determines what you *have*. Your experiences come from your beliefs.

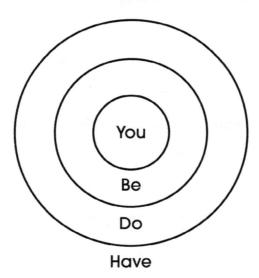

If you want to *have* the *experience* of freedom in water, your beliefs need to support this. This next exercise puts in motion the process to change your beliefs.

Go through this list again. After each belief, rewrite it, stating clearly what you *want* to believe.

If I put my face in water, I'll get water in my nose or mouth.

_____

It's dangerous when I get water in my nose or mouth.

_____

If I get water in my nose or mouth, I'll struggle, sputter, cough, and possibly drown.

_____

If water gets into my mouth, I'll swallow it.

_____

If I relax in water, I'll drop straight to the bottom like a stone.

_____

Sometimes I can't keep my presence of mind in deep water.

_____

I am not a floater.

_____

I know I can float.

_____

I am not a swimmer yet.

_____

I was born a swimmer.

_____

It would be unwise of me to relax in water.

_____

I have to push myself in order to learn to swim.

If I relax in water, I might lose control.

I may not have adequate lung capacity to swim.

Deep water works differently than shallow water.

My mind works differently in deep water than it does in shallow water.

It would be unwise of me to relax in deep water.

If I relax in deep water, something dreadful will happen.

Each breath I take must be maximal in case I don't get another one.

I can't control my body well in deep water.

If a skill works in the shallow end, it won't necessarily work in the deep end.

If I want to learn to swim, I have to follow the swimming instructor's directions, even if I don't want to.

To float correctly, my body should be horizontal.

Being able to float depends on where the bottom is.

Being able to do other skills depends on where the bottom is.

A person can't get air if s/he's in deep water because there's no bottom to stand on.

When I'm in deep water, I must move vigorously to stay afloat.

In deep water, I need skills that I don't need in shallow water.

In order to rest, I need the bottom or the side.

It's harder to breathe in deep water than in shallow water.

Shallow water is as dangerous as deep water.

Shallow water won't hold me up.

Deep water won't hold me up.

The water is more powerful than I am.

_____

I need to be more physically fit than I am to learn to swim.

_____

This book may work for others, but it may not work for me.

_____

I don't trust myself in deep water.

_____

Other beliefs:

_____

_____

By becoming aware of these beliefs—both the ones you have and the ones you want to have—a slight shift takes place. Can you feel it? It's a physical shift. Even though your body may not have "moved," something inside you moved the tiniest bit. This is a change at the "being" level. Change has begun.

STEP 23: YOUR FACE

"Last night I put my face in the shower for the first time in my life!"
—Annabella, Age 56

Question: What do you do if you drop the soap in the shower?

Answer: Kick it to the other end of the tub and get it.

How do you feel at the thought of putting your face in the water? Feel your body's reaction. If you tense up, feel where the tension is. Feel it for a minute. Then rest.

Think again about putting your face in, and let the tension be there. When you let it be there, what happens? Let it be there until it lessens and then disappears. Go slowly and be gentle. Don't push.

Without getting into the water, you can practice putting your face in by repeatedly thinking about it, feeling your reaction, and allowing it. If it sounds like fun, repeat this until it doesn't bother you. Don't push.

What are your concerns, if any, about having your face in water? Here are some common ones:

- Water in the nose
- Water in the eyes
- Water in the mouth
- Water in the ears
- Inhaling under water
- Running out of air
- Losing balance
- Losing control/panicking
- Not being able to come up in time for air
- Feeling claustrophobic

Let's take care of every single one of these.

WE DON'T CARE IF YOU ACTUALLY PUT YOUR FACE IN

When I say "we," I mean "you and I." What we care about is that you feel completely in control. Do you agree?

MAKING IT SAFE TO PUT YOUR FACE IN

Look at a second hand on a watch or clock. If you can hold your breath for five seconds, can you imagine feeling safe putting your face in the water for one second? Take a breath and time how long you can hold it.

This gives you an idea of how long you can comfortably have your face in the water. For almost all of the skills you learn in this book in which your face is in the water, you'll be holding your breath. This is the best way for you to come to know your lung capacity and the amount of time you can "play" on that much air. Later in the book we'll introduce breathing, but for now, just become very familiar with holding your breath. Always keep it comfortable. Don't push yourself at all. In fact, I'm counting on you *not* to.

Please don't expect to remember all the steps below when you go to the pool. Get the idea of what is meant as you read, and then do what your body tells you when you're at the pool. In case you get stuck, you may want to take the book along. You can also practice some of these skills in a tub that's not too hot. Ninety-five degrees Fahrenheit (35° C) is okay. One hundred and two degrees (hot tub) is rather hot for your face (39° C).

Do all of the following, which will help you to feel 100% safe putting your face in the water. Doing fewer of the following is not more advanced than doing all of them. The most advanced state is feeling 100% in control: zero discomfort.
- Hold onto the wall or gutter with one hand
- Hold your nose
- Take a breath
- Close your mouth
- Close your eyes
- Slowly lower your face down toward the water. There's no need to put your ears under water but if you want to, it's okay.

- As you approach the water's surface, ask yourself if putting your face in is what you really want to do (if it sounds like fun). If some part of you says, "No," then come back up. Take a break. When you feel rested, start again. Repeat this cycle as many times as necessary until you reach the point where you want to put your face in. *We don't care if you put your face in.* We only care that you're practicing staying in control. The more you practice control, the better you'll be at remaining in control. After a while, you become expert at remaining in control. And after that, you'll feel free and safe to put your face in.
- If you want to put your face in, then hold your breath and slowly lower your face into the water, keeping your hand on your nose and your eyes and mouth closed. Spend a moment there if it's comfortable.
- Come up whenever you want to. Don't push yourself to stay in. You may be there for one second. If this feels like enough for you, it is enough. Practice this many, many times, as many as you enjoy.

HOLDING AIR IN YOUR CHEEKS

Often, as someone prepares to go under water, he holds air in his cheeks.

Cheeks full of air (with a bubble sneaking out).

Getting ready to submerge, he's sure he wants air,
but the air he needs isn't in his cheeks.

The air in your cheeks isn't available for your body to use. It just puffs up your cheeks. The air you live on is in your lungs. So, when you take a breath and hold it, feel it in your lungs. Your face doesn't have to work.

CLAUSTROPHOBIA IN THE WATER

Some students feel closed-in or trapped under water. Our claustrophobic students have all overcome their fear of putting their faces in water. You may not believe me now, and that's fine.

It's true that you can't breathe in with your face in the water. You can breathe out if you wish (but it's not necessary now). Your lungs can hold so much air that there's plenty to live on for every exercise we will do. Later you'll learn that it's hard to get rid of all your air even if you want to.

I won't try to talk you out of claustrophobia. I just ask you to listen to your feelings and experiment with the steps provided at your own pace. Stay true to yourself.

Your lungs can hold enough air for you to go into the water and come back up and still have loads of air left. Are you willing to test this?

You can heal the sensation of claustrophobia in the water. Follow your instinct. If it says, "Don't go in," don't go in. Just go *as far as you feel completely comfortable* going. Make sure you hold onto the wall. Make sure you hold your nose. Allow yourself to do only what is comfortable. Give yourself many days to learn to put your face in. Let go of a timetable. If you stay in your body and let go of a schedule, you'll get it.

STEP 24: THE NECESSITY OF BEING IN CONTROL

WHY IT'S MORE IMPORTANT TO BE IN CONTROL THAN TO DO A SKILL

People have asked, "Are you sure you don't want me to force my face in, just to get it done?" Yes, I'm sure.

Why put your face in if you don't want to? You don't have to do things you don't like to do in order to learn to swim. If you did, why would you want to learn to swim? You'd be practicing the 3rd Circle, which is not a skill or a behavior you want to learn.

You're already experienced enough at pushing and losing control. Our goal is to experience control and comfort. You're reading this book because you want to know how to be in control all the time in the water, shallow and deep, in the middle or at the side, at the surface or the bottom of the pool, and perhaps in the lake or ocean. You want to be in control whether someone splashes you or not, jumps in right next to you, bumps into you, or whether you walk off a drop-off or fall from a dock or boat. True?

You may have been taught that you would get control by learning swim skills. The truth is, you'll get control by practicing control. You build confidence in your ability to stay in control by starting with little successes and building on them. You'll swim when you feel so in-control that you have attention to spare for moving.

Practice putting your face in the water 50 to 100 times, as described several pages back. Give yourself all the time in the world. You aren't in a hurry, are you? If so, you're at least in the 2nd Circle. This won't work in the long run. Stop and come back home to your body.

2+2=4

TO LEARN, YOU MUST BE ABLE TO DO STEP 1 AND REMAIN IN THE 1ST CIRCLE EVERY TIME BEFORE YOU CAN ADD STEP 2.

WHAT IS YOUR FACE DOING?

Once you've had your face in water for a while, notice your expression under water. What are the sensations in your face? Your forehead? Eyes? Cheeks? Lips? Jaw?

Tension is okay: find it, feel it, and *let it be there*. Catch yourself if you're thinking, "I should relax." Having tension in your face uses energy and attention, even if you don't notice it. If some of your attention and energy are in your face, then *all of you* can't be learning the next step. Let all your attention be in your face while your face requires it. It's okay; go with it.

If you ever feel stuck during this learning process, check back to see if you're in the 1st Circle. If there's tension, meaning you're in the 2nd or 3rd Circle, you won't be able to advance in that skill. Go back and find where any tension is, and *let it be there*. Don't expect progress unless and until you've allowed it fully, which gives it its first chance to disappear.

Are You Swallowing While You're Under Water?

Sometimes, people find themselves swallowing when they put their faces in the water. This is okay. They're not swallowing water…they're simply swallowing. If you find yourself swallowing, let it happen. There's no harm in it. By allowing it, you'll eventually see what you're doing to cause it. Later, when you have more control, it will stop by itself.

This is "honest learning" as I call it, an organic change that happens naturally and without force.

While we're on the topic of swallowing, let's establish this: if you do find yourself swallowing water, it's not dangerous. It just goes into your stomach. You can swallow a lot of water, even many gulps in a row if things are not going as planned, and not be in danger from the water intake. If you're swallowing water because you're out of control, it's being out of control that could lead to danger, not the water intake. Once again, being in control is the key skill to learn.

Obviously, if you're in water that's not clean, you wouldn't want to swallow it. You shouldn't even get into it. If you have a sense that the water at the pool isn't clean, or if you're not sure, don't get in. It's okay to ask, though you could get an odd look.

If you're in the ocean, swallowing a lot of saltwater can be distressing and may make you nauseous after a while. Remember that this happens when you aren't in control. This is why it's so important to be comfortable. When you learn to be in your body, it's unlikely that swallowing water will happen anymore.

STEP 25: PUTTING YOUR EARS IN

It's safe to get water in your ears. For all intents and purposes, your ears are like side pockets in your head. Water won't go into your brain, nose, or throat. If you're not comfortable putting your ears in water, follow this recipe:

- Hold onto the wall with one or both hands.
- Tip your head sideways, parallel to the surface.
- Lower your head.
- As you approach the surface with one ear, ask yourself whether you want to put your ear in the water or not. Is there any tension in your body telling you "No"? If so, come up and take a break.
- If not, here's a preview of putting your ear in. Your ear will fill with water, which may tickle. Your hearing will change; sounds will be muffled in that ear.
- You can just touch your earlobe to the water and see how that feels. If you don't like the idea of submersing your ear, come back up and take a break. Don't force yourself to put your ear in.
- Once you're willing to put your ear in, see how it feels. See how *your body* feels with your ear in. Come up whenever you want.

> WE DON'T CARE IF YOU PUT YOUR EAR IN
> THE WATER. WE ONLY CARE THAT YOU REMAIN
> IN CONTROL AND HAVE FUN.

When you get into the water to actually try this, I hope you won't say to yourself, "Oh, I can skip that step. She doesn't really mean that." I am giving you the tried and true, the guaranteed-to-be-successful steps. If you want to give yourself the best possible chance for success, follow the steps. If you *know* that you don't need a step though, trust yourself. You're right.

Once you've become comfortable with submersing one ear, follow the same steps with your other ear. Take your time. Don't push yourself. Remain in the 1st Circle.

HOW TO GET WATER OUT OF YOUR EARS

Sometimes, water doesn't all drain out of your ears when you come to the surface. Shaking your head usually gets rid of it. If a gentle shake doesn't do it, then:

- Move your head quickly in one direction and then stop it. The water will keep going.
- If that doesn't clear your ears, go back under water and fill your ears again. Come back up and try the same thing.
- If that doesn't clear them, put a drop of mineral oil in your ear. Use only mineral oil. Lie on your side with your head on a pillow (or not) and wait 5 minutes. It should clear.

TAKING CARE OF YOUR EARS

After swimming, allow your ears to dry. If you have long hair, put it behind your ears until they air-dry. You would not want to place your head down on a pillow and go to sleep when your ear is still wet. You could wake up with swimmer's ear, a fungal infection. If you need to dry your ears quickly, remember the saying: "Never put anything smaller than your elbow in your ear." Hold a hair dryer at arm's length from your ear and direct the air toward it.

When you feel okay about putting each of your ears in, hold the wall and ask yourself if you're ready to try putting the back of your head under water far enough that both ears go in. If that doesn't sound like fun, don't do it. Simply feel where the tension is in your body when you imagine it. Let yourself feel that tension. Don't try to make it disappear; it is protecting you. When you've let it be there, the tension will start to melt away. This is simply the way healing fear works. If you're in a hurry, you'll delay your learning. If it's not time to put your ears in, that's fine. Take the easy route.

2+2=4
WHEN YOU ALLOW TENSION TO BE THERE, IT HAS ITS FIRST OPPORTUNITY TO DISAPPEAR—AND IT WILL.

We don't know if it will leave right now or not, but at least you're giving it a chance. You aren't in control of when it disappears. You just have to allow it. Then it will go. This is an "energy law"— one of the laws that govern the way energy works. This is why it's important not to be in a hurry when you learn. You, a spirit, are energy.

TENSION IS A COMMUNICATION

When your body is tense, you're receiving a message from your beliefs that you may not be safe. It would be crazy to proceed if you actually are not safe. The part of you that believes you're not safe is the part that's learning and overcoming fear. To overcome fear, you must pay attention to the beliefs and tension. When the afraid part of you believes that you're safe because you're listening to it and letting tension be there, tension disappears. Your belief starts to change. You grow. Listen to your body. It's the communication channel between your wisdom and you.

Have you ever been told by swimming teachers and family members to relax in the water?

Being told to relax is practically a joke for afraid students.

If you try to make tension disappear ("RELAX!"), it usually persists. *What you resist persists.*

We don't want you to be tense, since tension means you're not having fun and you're in the 2nd Circle or beyond. At the same time, we don't want you to tell yourself to relax because sometimes that helps you relax and sometimes it makes you more tense. We need a system that gives you the best chance of returning to the 1st Circle every single time.

The system to learn is this: let yourself be the way you are. By letting yourself be tense, your resistance to tension goes away. Then, your tension can also go away. This is a most effective solution. It heals.

If at some time in the future you find yourself in a frightening situation and you *cannot* make yourself relax, you will still be able to pull through because you will have developed a far more dependable habit: letting yourself be the way you are. Practice it.

You'll automatically begin to relax once you allow what's already happening to happen. Tension is okay. Trusting it will heal it. Don't be in a hurry to change. The change happens by itself when you're in your body. Change doesn't happen if you're next to your body, pushing. *I know I've said this many times.* Hopefully you're learning it. If I've said it too much, pardon me.

STEP 26: COMPARING YOURSELF TO OTHERS

To compare yourself to others, or to compare yourself to your vision of where you "should be," is to be outside of yourself, looking back at yourself. Being outside of your body, you're in no position to learn. You may even be in an attack position, ready to judge yourself if you don't measure up to someone else. Will this help you learn?

If you're comparing yourself, bring yourself back into your body and feel your feelings. Impatience? Sadness? Tension? Hurry? Just be still and feel them. They have a place in your learning and healing. Just feel as much as you feel safe to feel. Let that energy/emotion be there. This is the definition of healing!

When you recover from comparing yourself, consider walking across the pool. You might imagine yourself holding onto the wall or doing whatever makes you feel safe. When you're ready to try it, go slowly, the safest way. Feel. Feel what it's like to be in the exact same place that your body is, to fill your body with your presence from head to toe and fingertip to fingertip. If you do this, you're likely to feel things you haven't felt before in water. You may feel your buoyancy. Sometimes people feel the resistance of the water, which is so much greater than that of air. Sometimes people feel how their balance is different than in air. All these are factors to learn about.

By being present, you'll notice things that have always been there. But you may have never been in your body to feel them.

STEP 27: OPENING YOUR EYES UNDER WATER

We don't care if you open your eyes or not. What we care about is that you feel in control and comfortable. Most people want to be able to see in the water. Many have never opened their eyes below the surface. If you wear goggles or a mask (to be described in a moment), opening your eyes under water is easy.

Many people want to know what it's like to open their eyes without goggles or a mask, so they'll be familiar with this feeling. They want to know that if they ever fall into the water without goggles, they won't "lose it." Good idea. If putting your eyes into the water and opening them sounds like no fun at all, skip this part for now. Keep them closed or wear goggles. Please do not pry your eyes open or force them. Simply let them open when they are ready.

When you put your face in water without goggles, notice whether there's tension in your eyes. Go ahead and see. If you find tension in your eyes, practice what you're learning: let it be there. Just feel the tension. Don't tell yourself to relax. Don't force your eyes open. When you have allowed tension to be there, what do you think will happen? Write it here:

_____

The tension in your eyes starts to disappear, or your eyes open. If not, feel and allow the tension again. You'll notice that it requires just the slightest bit of tension to keep your eyes closed. If you allow *that* tension, what happens? Your eyes open *on their own*. You can see. It will be blurry, but you can see.

How does it feel on your eyeballs to open your eyes? Only open them as much as you want to. It's just for fun. It won't hurt you. The view is blurry because there's no air space in front of your eyes. If you were to wear goggles, your vision would be as clear as it is in the air. Look around under water. Can you see people's legs? The colors of their suits? The number of fingers I'm holding up? Just kidding.

If you were to leave your eyes open for 5-10 minutes in most chlorinated pools, they might burn a little bit from the chemical balance. This doesn't cause damage, but it can be uncomfortable. This is one reason many people use goggles. They provide good vision and comfort for your eyes. Pools that have ozonated water—and therefore less chlorine—don't sting your eyes.

It's good to spend some time in the pool with your face in the water and your eyes open every day so it becomes natural and comfortable. After it becomes second nature to you to open your eyes under water, you may wish to get a pair of goggles (see below). It's fine to spend all your time in the water without goggles, but they make it possible to see much better. Seeing clearly gives more control.

GLASSES

If you can't see well without your glasses and taking them off makes you uncomfortable in the water, there are several things you can do.

- Wear them in the pool. This works while you're above the surface.
- Wear contacts under goggles.
- Purchase goggles that have your prescription ground into the lenses.

STEP 28: MAKE IT SIMPLE FOR YOURSELF

It won't hurt you to make things simple. This will assist you in being in your body, which is the whole point. Make *everything* simple. There is no such thing as "cheating" as you learn to swim. Get the basic concerns out of the way (fear, cold, water in your nose…). When you don't have to worry about these things, you can learn what you want to know. Comfort comes first.

CHOOSING AND USING A NOSE CLIP

A nose clip is a small device that keeps water out of your nose, frees your hands, and therefore gives you more control. Many people think of it as a crutch. Others consider it "cheating." In truth, it's neither a crutch nor cheating; it helps you to be in your body. Why not make it easy for yourself? A nose clip is a steppingstone. You'll stop using it when the time is right, when you don't need it anymore.

A nose clip can be anything from a clothespin to an $15 colored designer item. Nose clips usually cost $3 to $5. Different brands have different shapes, and one will fit your nose better than others. Nose clips will fall off if you have sun block or moisturizer on your nose. You may have to invest a few dollars and use trial and error to find the best one.

Once you have a nose clip, test it to make sure it stays on your face and no water enters your nose. Found a good one? Buy two. Please give yourself permission to use a nose clip if it will help you stay in your body. It's more important to stay in control than to be nose-clip-free.

Choosing Goggles

Goggles are small, enclosed glasses that provide air space in front of your eyes so you can see clearly. There are hundreds of models of goggles on the market. They fit all kinds of faces. A great pair for me could be a pair that doesn't work at all for you. Find a pair that fits your face comfortably and doesn't leak. Test it in the pool.

To find a pair of goggles, go to a swimming-supply or sporting goods store and ask if they have unpackaged goggles you can try on. If not, they may let you open packages.

Placing the goggles against your face without the strap around your head, press them into your eye sockets and see if they create suction. If they do, they are likely to fit you. If they are the type that doesn't rely on suction, it will say so on the package; follow the instructions for fitting. Most goggles are the suction type.

If you want vision correction in your goggles, there are models that are ground to a certain diopter. You can buy them over the counter at many swimming-gear and sporting goods stores. Some optometrists grind goggles to match your exact prescription. Check to see which models can be ground, then choose one that fits your face.

There are also several types of masks, larger and for some people more comfortable than goggles, that don't cover the nose. Ask to try on a swimmer's mask. You can't be sure until you get into the pool whether or not a pair will be leak-proof. Ask at the store about their return policy.

Once you begin to wear goggles, review from time to time opening your eyes under water without them. This helps you to practice control without goggles. If you were ever to find yourself in the water without goggles, you'd want to know that you wouldn't lose control just because you didn't have them.

Once you find a pair of goggles that fits, buy two.

Using goggles and a nose clip really made a difference for me and made me feel very comfortable. —Joseph

STEP 29: THE SPIRITUAL SIDE OF LEARNING

THERE'S NO SUCH THING AS "STUCK"

All things in the universe are composed of energy in one form or another. Your body is energy, your thoughts are energy, sound and light are energy, information is energy, emotion is energy. Your chair is energy.

Energy does only two things: it expands and contracts. Everything in the universe expands and contracts. Though you may not be able to detect it, your chair expands and contracts in a rhythm of its own. Your heart expands and contracts in its own rhythm. So do the molecules of this page. And though we don't yet have instruments sophisticated enough to measure them, your moods and learning expand and contract in their own rhythm.

You may say, "I've experienced my energy expanding when I feel good. I feel myself contracting when I feel bad. But I have also felt stuck. Isn't that a third thing energy does?" No. "Stuck" can only happen if there's contraction. Energy keeps expanding unless there's contraction.

Contraction is part of the cycle of learning. It's not bad or good: it just is. We contract when it's necessary to "keep ourselves safe" according to our beliefs.

How does this relate to your swimming? When you're in the water and you're worried, how does your body feel? What does it do? It contracts, gets tense. Your chin may come down, your shoulders may hunch up, and your chest, throat, arms, legs, and jaw may tighten.

On the other hand, when you're in water and you feel safe, how does your body feel? You're relaxed, expanded. You feel looser, more at ease. You expand your body by thinking calming, soothing thoughts. You contract by thinking scary, threatening thoughts.

You may have never thought of having control over which thoughts you had in the water. And you may not have had any. But today, please open to this possibility: when you're on land and you notice yourself having scary thoughts and tensing up, check your thoughts. Are those the thoughts you want to have? If yes, fine. If no, fine. Are they based in truth? If yes, fine. If no, fine. Be aware that you have a choice about what you want to think next.

When you're in the water and you find yourself becoming tense, check your thoughts. Are those the thoughts you want to have? Are they based in truth? Either way is fine. Just be aware that you have a choice.

I'm not asking you to talk yourself out of being tense. I am asking you to be present. You can steer your thoughts out of the encroaching grip of panic if you let yourself stop. To steer your thoughts is to change your "location." It's simply another tool in your toolbox to bring you closer to the truth about yourself in the water. You are non-physical. Your thoughts determine whether you expand or contract. Your body and your thoughts together give you fabulous clay with which to mold the swimmer you were born to be. This molding can happen with fun and very little effort.

GO SLOWLY ENOUGH THAT YOU CAN CHOOSE

EXERCISE: PRESENCE

Where are you now? Are you in your body? Are you partly in your body and partly somewhere else? Are you totally "gone?" No; you'd have to reread the paragraph if you were gone.

Here is an exercise you could record into your phone and play back:

- Bring your focus into your body fully. Feel what it's like to be totally "home." Is this where you spend most of your day? Any of your day? (Just kidding.)
- Now close your eyes and feel yourself sitting in your seat. Be aware of your sitting position, the clothes you're wearing, the way they feel on your body, and your sensations.
- Now pretend that you're across the room looking back at your body.
- It's sitting in the chair. See the position it's in and what it's wearing. Then, bring yourself back into your body again. You're home again.
- How does it feel?
- Now imagine yourself again across the room, looking back at your body sitting in the chair. Look at it from across the room.
- Now return to your body again and feel what it's like to be in it.

It feels different to be in your body than to be across the room looking back at it. Did you feel this? This helps you learn the different feelings between being in your body and out of it. Don't worry if you weren't able to do it. Not everyone can.

When you're in the water, you can keep your self in your body by *feeling*. Feel how the water embraces every inch of your body. Feel how it buffets you ever so slightly back and forth or holds you as you simply stay still. Feel your arms' lightness in the water. Feel how much air you have. By keeping your attention (your focus, yourself) in your body, you remain in the present, in control. It's simple. It works.

There is more to the spiritual side of learning. We have touched on some of it. The physical side includes your body, gravity, buoyancy, the amount of air you hold. The spiritual side includes your presence, how energy works, your beliefs, thoughts, and feelings. It includes your compassion toward yourself and your permission to go slowly. More on these later.

For those who are challenged by this message, here is one student's comment:

It sounds like b--------, but it works. —Tim

STEP 30: PUTTING YOUR FACE IN WITHOUT HOLDING YOUR NOSE

When you put your face in the water earlier, you either held your nose or you didn't. If you did, and you'd like to keep your nose sealed off, you can either hold it again or use a nose clip. If you hold your nose, it will obviously be safe. However, using your hand occupies that hand.

If you prefer not to use a nose clip, you can learn to keep water out of your nose in front float positions. Holding your nose, put your face in the water as you have been doing it. Once there, while you're feeling completely in control—and if it sounds like fun—add one new thing: release your grip on your nose, keeping your hand in the very same spot. Don't change anything but that one small thing: letting go of your nose. You won't get water in your nose. You won't inhale, because you're present and you're only doing one thing. You'll find that it's safe to have your nose unplugged in the water.

Note: if you're thinking you don't want to use a nose clip because in the long run you don't want to wear one, please reconsider. Today is not the long run. Today is "comfort priority day." Do what will make you most comfortable today. What you want for the long run will take care of itself.

When you take your hand off your nose under water, the pressure of your fingers on your nose goes away (I don't mean to be too elementary here). Your nostrils fill with water. This is not the same as "getting water in your nose." Having your nostrils fill with water is possibly a new sensation and for some people it takes a few minutes of practice for several days to get used to it. When water takes up the space in your nostrils, it fills your nostrils, just as it would fill an empty glass if you placed it in the water. See if the sensation is okay with you. Get accustomed to this new feeling.

Please be kind to yourself. There's no hurry. Practice having your face under water with your fingers half an inch from your nose. If you feel comfortable with that, and you know that you won't inhale because you're in control, feel what it's like to have your face in water, nose open. Practice this thirty times. One hundred times. No hurry.

When you become comfortable having your nose free, you'll be able to move your hand away from your face and know that your nose is safe. Your nose is safe because you know what you're doing: you're *there*.

TAKE CARE OF YOUR NOSE

The sensation of "getting water in your nose" is actually getting water in your sinuses. The bones around your nose form a circle at the top of your nose, beyond which your sinuses lie. If water goes beyond this circle, it enters your sinuses. We want to avoid this whenever possible because it's quite uncomfortable.

You would not want to become accustomed to the discomfort of getting water in your sinuses because:
1) if you are uncomfortable, you're a step closer to the 5th Circle
2) too much water in the nose (sinuses) can cause a sinus infection

Smile. You can prevent water from going beyond the circle at the back of your nose and into your sinuses.

STEP 31: HOW TO KEEP WATER OUT OF YOUR NOSE

If your face is tilted straight ahead or straight down in the water, all the water in your nostrils will stay in your nostrils and cause no discomfort. If your head is in one of the following positions, you will not get water into your sinuses (your "nose") unless, of course, you inhale— in other words, if you're not home. Safe positions for your nose:

These positions of your head are safe for your nose

However, if you…

   1) turn upside down,

   2) do a somersault,

   3) look upward while under water, or

   4) put your head back too far while you're in a back float, then the water sitting in your nostrils will go into your sinuses unless you know how to prevent it. You'll probably come up and sneeze.

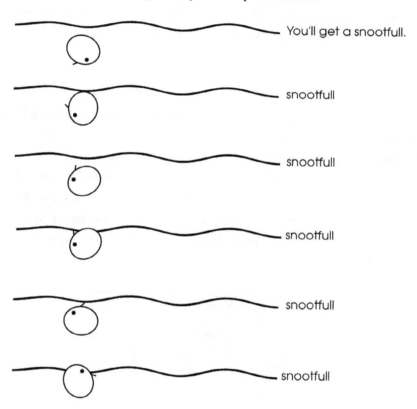

You'll get a snootfull.

snootfull

snootfull

snootfull

snootfull

snootfull

Uncomfortable positions for your nose:
If your head is in any of these positions, you will get a snootfull.

You can prevent water in your nose by:

   • Not tipping your head backward and not putting it upside down

   • Not inhaling when you're under water (this means you must "be there")

- Not moving your nose through the water like a scoop
- Using a nose clip
- Holding your nose
- Exhaling through your nose anytime your head is tipped backward or upside down. It's completely safe and comfortable to be upside down or turning somersaults in the water. You won't get water in your nose *if*, as you turn, you exhale through your nose the whole time. The air coming out of your nose will prevent water from coming in. Exhaling through your mouth will not keep water out of your nose.

BLIPPING

Here is way to keep water out of your nose when you put your face in. Inhale through your mouth above the surface, then exhale a little bit of air through your nose as you put your face in. Stop exhaling after your nose is below the surface. I call this sending out a "blip" of air. Just a few bubbles outward prevent you from getting water in. If you "blip" each time you put your face in and take it out, you'll prevent water from coming into your nose. If you don't blip, you may not get water into your nose, either. But if you want to ensure no water, blip.

Blipping: just exhale a couple of bubbles, then stop.

Give yourself lots of time to become comfortable with blipping: days.

This habit of blipping to keep water out of your nose is worth every minute you put into it. I urge you to give yourself enough time to practice and embody it or give yourself permission to use a nose clip (unless water isn't entering your sinuses). Prevent discomfort.

Once you can have your hands free of your nose and you're at ease with your face in the water, you'll be ready for another step. But don't try to move on until you're happy having your face and ears in the water.

KEEP YOUR NOSE HAPPY AT ALL TIMES

STEP 32: REVIEW

Every time you get into the water, review the basics you have already covered. Remove expectations that you can pick up where you left off last time: that would be a mistake!

Then practice:
1. noticing how you feel

2. allowing yourself to be "where you are" today with no expectations of repeating what you did yesterday

3. letting yourself be yourself

4. putting your face in

5. putting your ears in

6. asking yourself if this is enough for today

7. doing whatever would be fun

8. if you're in the mood to continue practicing, then practice...

9. taking your hand off your nose

10. opening your eyes under water

Step 33: Feel the Water Hold You Up: the Front Float

Once you're comfortable (in the 1st Circle) putting your face and ears in the water, you may wish to learn how to float. The first step of floating is feeling that the water holds you up. To assure yourself that you're safe, hold onto the wall and *don't let go*...unless, of course, you're already comfortable without the wall.

DON'T EVEN THINK ABOUT LETTING GO OF THE WALL.

"This is one swimming class where they encourage
you not to let go of the wall."
—KTVU News, Oakland, CA, 1995

One thing to know about the front float: your feet may be on the floor in shallow water. Though most people don't believe this is correct, it is, if it's where your feet go without effort. More on that later.

Face the wall and hold onto it with both hands. Promise yourself you won't let go.

Take a comfortable breath. When you're ready, put your face in the water and let your body dangle freely as you hold onto the wall. Let your feet be on the floor. Don't try to make your body be horizontal or lift your feet off the floor. If they float up by themselves, that's fine. If not, fine. Do you believe me? You don't have to push yourself into a horizontal position. You don't have to push yourself below the surface, either. Just lie there limply, letting your body dangle while holding onto the wall. The more air you have the higher you'll float. If you can leave your feet on the floor, do so.

Here is a picture of a good front float by someone who is allowing the water to do all the work.

A good front float at the wall

A FLOAT DOES *NOT* HAVE TO BE HORIZONTAL

Contrary to popular belief, a good float is not "supposed to be" horizontal, whether it's a front float or a back float. Check your resistance to that statement. A good front float is one in which the water does all the work and your body does none. All you do is hold your breath. For some people (some bodies), the float will be horizontal.

Another good front float, though a bit stiff

Some people float vertically:

Another good front float

Some people may not float:

**A person who takes a big breath and promptly parks on the floor
on her/his knees is likely a sinker. This swimmer sank by exhaling
her air. However, not everyone who exhales their air can sink.**

Very few people sink: for them, a float will not work. Most non-swimmers believe they're sinkers. Most likely, you're not one. We'll talk about sinking in a moment.

WHY SOME PEOPLE FLOAT HORIZONTALLY AND OTHERS DON'T

The position you float in is determined by your body composition. Any parts of your body that are lighter than water—less dense—will float. Any parts that are heavier than water—denser—will sink. The two things in our bodies that are lighter than water are air and fat. The two things in our bodies that are heavier than water are muscle and bone. If you have a lot of air in your lungs, you'll be more buoyant than if you have just a little.

If you have a high proportion of fat relative to your total body weight, the effect will be that you float higher: perhaps horizontally. If you have a high proportion of muscle, you'll float diagonally or vertically. If you have a lot of muscle and bone relative to your body weight, your feet will sink to the bottom in shallow water. Very dense bodies sink if allowed to. This *need not be an emergency.*

The water is one place where those extra desserts can come in handy...if you're attached to floating, that is.

YOUR NORMAL, GOOD FLOAT

Which of the floats above is yours? During your float, once you're comfortable, place one hand on the back of your head and feel it in the air. Are you surprised? Did you think you were under water? Spend time absorbing that. If you're a sinker, you will be under water. It's okay, if it's okay with you!

YOU DON'T HAVE TO BE A HORIZONTAL FLOATER, OR A FLOATER AT ALL TO BE A GOOD SWIMMER

When you hold onto the wall and put your face in the water, do you kick your feet up in the belief that they are supposed to float and that you're supposed to be horizontal? This has become a habit of many people who have tried to learn to float. However, it's wasted energy to kick the feet up, as they will either sink on their own or float on their own. Your effort will not bring you to your natural float. Your natural float, the effortless float, is a perfectly good float and the correct one for you. It will be different from the next person's. Again: when you hold onto the wall, place your face in the water and hold your breath. Let yourself dangle in the water and see how it holds you. Don't let go of the wall. Your hands' purpose will be to keep you from drifting away from the wall, not to hold you up. Let the water hold your body up. This is how you'll feel your float, perhaps for the first time.

IF YOU WANT TO GET TECHNICAL

When you walk or do things on land, your body moves around a point called your center of gravity. You remain in balance. When you move in water, your body moves around a point called your center of buoyancy. Yes, there's balance in the water, too.

When your center of gravity and your center of buoyancy are vertically aligned, you reach your natural, effortless floating position. If they're the same point, you float horizontally.

If you experiment with taking a bigger breath, your floating position will become more horizontal. Why? Right, because you will have caused your center of buoyancy to move toward your head. If you experiment with putting your arms or feet in different places while you float, your floating position will change, too; your center of gravity changes when you redistribute your weight.

WHAT I MEAN WHEN I SAY, "DON'T LET GO OF THE WALL"

When I say don't let go of the wall, I mean keep your fingers around the gutter and hold it with absolutely no intention of letting go, even partially.

Sometimes people think I mean, "see how little you can hold onto the wall" or "slip your fingers away little by little and see if you still feel safe" or "let go of one hand if you can." I don't mean these. If you did these, your attention would be on your fingers and the part of them that's touching the wall. Therefore, you would not feel the float or your buoyancy. Hold onto the wall in such a way that you grasp it and keep it.

Let's say you're at the wall and you're thinking that the water might hold you up. You're ready to let go for a moment: you want to test it. You raise your hands off the gutter and poise them above it, ready to grasp it again "in case something happens." When you raise your hands out of the water, they are no longer floating: they're in the air. If they're in the air, the weight of them will push you down a little bit, depending on how far out of the water they are. If they're a few inches out, you'll feel the weight push you down. If you put them higher up, you'll sink lower. When you feel yourself sinking a little bit, you may have the thought that by letting go of the wall, you'll sink. This is not true. You would continue to float, but you'd dip under for a second.

Let's say you leave your hands on the gutter or wall and then slide them into the water. You'd remain floating at the same level you were at when you were holding on. You'd find that the water holds you up even when you let go. You would not want to try this if you might leave your body, however.

Sometimes when I watch someone let go of the wall this way, her hands are shaking. This is not a sign of joy. Shaking hands mean fear. The student has made letting go of the wall her goal, rather than staying comfortable.

If your hands are shaking, you've forgotten that comfort is the goal:

- your focus is no longer in your body: it's at the wall or at the bottom. This means *you* are at the wall or at the bottom.

- you're trying to float *before* you know that the water is doing the work. This is not a good idea. It takes you to the 2nd or 3rd Circle. This prevents you from feeling the water hold you up. *It's essential to feel what the water does for you.* If your hands are shaking, you are surely not in the 1st Circle. Slow down. Feel the float until you know the water is holding you—at least your upper body—up.

On the other hand, if you're so curious about letting go of the wall that it would be more comfortable to try it than not to, lifting your hands above the wall won't cause your hands to shake; you'll be in your body. Go ahead.

KIDDIE POOLS

The very best place to learn to float on your own is in a very shallow pool such as a kiddie pool including an inflatable back yard kiddie pool—one to two feet deep—or on wide, shallow steps. This can save you months of effort. If learning on steps, use only wide steps when there aren't many people entering and exiting the pool. Place your hands on the bottom of the pool or on a shallow step. Hold your breath and lower yourself down into the water. Let your feet be on the floor. If they float up, fine. Leave your hands on the bottom. How far down can you lower yourself into the water? Come up anytime.

**Learning at shallow steps. She feels the water
hold her up because she feels safe.**

As you let yourself down into the water—it will only allow you to lower yourself so far—feel what's happening. Does the water support you? How do you feel? Are you quiet inside? If not, feel your internal speed. Stay comfortable.

AFRICAN AMERICANS AND SWIMMING

Student Kelly, floating happily in the deep end, had the thought, "What am I doing here? We don't swim." If, like Kelly, you are African American or a person of color, take stock of the family and cultural messages about swimming that influenced you. Learning to float is a good time to start to address this. Write those messages here:

_____

_____

A book could be written about this alone. African Americans and any persons of color can learn to swim as well as anyone.

BECOMING FREE OF THE BOTTOM IN THE KIDDIE POOL

Feel as much as you can. Make it easy and fun. After awhile, when you feel the water doing all the work, lift your hands off the bottom an inch, where they'll feel safe. Are you floating? If you feel wobbly, feel the tension in your neck: you're probably holding your head up.

The very best place to learn to float: two feet of water

Practice feeling the water hold you up. Become convinced of it. You don't have to hold your feet up. Let the water *do everything*. Can you do anything to make the water *not* hold you? Try it, if you feel confident. Can you sink to the bottom in a foot of water? I challenge you to sink!

THE NEXT BEST THING TO A KIDDIE POOL

The next best thing to a kiddie pool is something that keeps you at the wall so you won't float away. Find a solid, stationary part of the pool, such as a railing, a rung of a pool ladder, a hook in the wall, or use a float bar (below). Connect yourself to it with my secure learn-to-float tether.

The tether keeps you securely connected to the railing, ladder, hook, or float bar, so you won't drift away. With the security of knowing you can stop when you wish, you can be comfortable and experiment. Distraction (the opposite of presence) is the thing that prevents someone from learning to float.

The tether, comprised of three straps, is adjustable. The short one connects securely to the rail. The long one is a belt. The other one gives you room to lie down in a front float.

Learn-to-float tether and Float Bar: patented[1]

With the tether on, make it short enough to keep you next to the rail. Then follow the steps given previously:

- Hold on to the wall, rail or ladder
- Take a breath
- Lower yourself into the water, happy to put your face in
- Let the water hold you up
- If you feel the water holding you up—if it sounds like fun—separate your fingers from the rail just a millimeter. Feel yourself floating.

The middle strap should be short enough that you can instantly reach the rail when you want to come up. No stretching to reach for it!

---

1   Learn-to-Float Bar and Tether available at MiracleSwimming.com.

Spend 30 minutes a day feeling the water hold you up. Become convinced of it. If it gets tiring, change the subject and come back another day. If you feel your upper body sinking, take a bigger breath next time.

Your toes or knees may be on the bottom. It's not "sinking;" it's your feet sinking. You might also float horizontally. Both are good!

Be sure the tether's length feels 100% safe. Practice pulling yourself back to the pole by the tether. If you need it to be shorter, connect the belt directly to the short strap.

TETHER PLACEMENT

Consider this. Fear has always been in the way of your learning to float and learning to swim. You cannot learn to swim while you're afraid—distracted by the very reasonable desire to feel safe.

You can learn beautifully and easily if you feel safe: reliably kept within reach of the side. If you don't have an instructor to keep you from drifting away, or a kiddie pool where you can put your hands on the bottom, the tether is what the doctor ordered. We should have thought of this decades ago!

The tether allows you to stay in your body—to feel safe—and therefore, to learn. You won't need it for long. But it's worth its weight in gold as you learn. Feeling safe is a step that cannot be skipped. The tether may temporarily "get in the way" of your face. Can you let it? Turn a bit.

Have someone else in the pool area with you any time you're in the water. This is a basic water safety rule.

On a short tether, he can easily reach safety. You can connect to a ladder.

Float Bar and Tether. Patented.

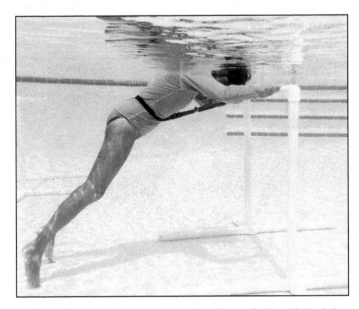

The tether keeps her close enough that she feels safe to let go:
she knows she can hold on and come up at will.

STEP 34: BECOME FREE OF THE SIDE: "UNFLOATING"

Give yourself days of practice feeling the water hold you up and getting used to the feeling of weightlessness. Unless you've been in space, this will be new. Don't even think about becoming free of the side until you are perfectly happy feeling yourself floating at the wall, holding on, in control.

Becoming free of the wall means you need to know how to stand up from a float. We call this unfloating.* If you're learning in water that's deeper than a kiddie pool or if the pool doesn't have shallow steps, then move to a place where you can put your hands around a railing or rail of a ladder. If there's no ladder, we'll cover that situation in a moment.

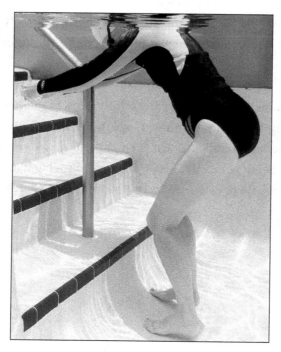

**Her fingers are clasped behind the ladder.
Your floating position may differ from this one.**

*A term created by Lynne

Hold onto the ladder below the surface and float. If you know the water is holding your body up—rather than your hands or feet— you can move your clasped fingers behind the ladder to avoid floating away, and feel the water doing all the work. You're floating. Grip the rail and come up whenever you want.

If you have the tether, you know you won't drift away and you can float with confidence.

THE RICHNESS OF EXPLORATION

My favorite way for a student to learn to unfloat at the wall is for him to be so in-his-body that the way to stand up simply comes to him. If you eliminate causes to worry and you explore and practice while you're calm, you can't help but learn on your own.

Answers just come to you when you're fully present, at ease, and in your body. By finding the solution yourself, you get "two for the price of one": the skill plus the self-confidence that even in the water, you can discover the answers by just being yourself. This is pure gold. Proving it to yourself is one of the best lessons there is. I encourage you to learn as much as you can by exploration.

To unfloat, use your abdominal muscles to pull your knees toward your chest. This is the unfloat, completed, using the ladder to keep you from drifting away.

As you become comfortable letting the water hold you up, in other words, when you know that it's the water holding you up, not your hands, the wall, or your feet, then you may be ready to notice other things. What do you notice? Do you know where your head is? Do you know where your limbs are relative to the surface? To the bottom? If this is too much to think about now, that's fine. You can return to it later.

Check to see if you're working. Why work? If you're not comfortable, you must have skipped a step and you need to go back to one that feels safe—one that allows you to be present.

STEPS OF UNFLOATING

1. Feel the water hold you up as you hold the wall or ladder.

2. Take time to feel that the water does all the work. Become convinced.

3. Remain in your body on purpose.

4. Remain in your body while you slowly bring your knees to your chest.

5. With your knees close to your chest, extend your feet forward and below your face and place them on the floor directly beneath your face.

6. Do this unfloat while holding the wall or ladder but without using it for support. Start the unfloat when you have plenty of air. Repeat this many times. Do it over many days until you own it.

7. When you can remain in your body for it, if it sounds like fun, let go of the wall or the ladder, remaining in control and unfloating. Repeat this until you've embodied it.

8. Unfloat away from the wall or ladder, remaining in control.

If pulling your knees under you using your abs doesn't quite do the trick, add a downward push with your hands on the wall. Later, you can push downward on the water and you'll receive the same effect. The water is thick and dense compared to air, so you can push on it.

If you have any hesitancy about unfloating, return to floating. Spend lots of time holding onto the wall, feeling the water hold you up. What is a lot of time? It's an hour. It's 4 hours. It's 20 minutes. It's so much time that you receive all the certainty in the world that you're being held up by the water and nothing else. Why stop before you're absolutely certain?

You may now have realized that letting the water hold you up and floating are the same thing.

Go slowly. We don't care if you unfloat. We only care that you feel comfortable. When you know you can be at ease letting go of the wall, unfloating will come naturally.

STEP 35: THE FRONT FLOAT AWAY FROM THE WALL

When you are comfortable letting go of the wall and drifting away a bit, or even beginning your front float in the middle of the pool, let yourself dangle in your float for a while. Notice that don't have to hold yourself up. You're letting the water do *everything*, right? When you do, you will find your natural float. This position is your unique position in the water based on your body composition: your aquatic signature, as it's called by Bill Boomer, stroke scientist extraordinaire.

One difference between floating at the wall and floating in the middle of the pool is that when you're away from the wall your hands won't float out in front of you; your arms will dangle wherever gravity takes them. The other difference is that if you're away from the wall, you need enough infrastructure to stay in your body. I'm sure you know this: don't float in the middle of the pool unless you know you can stay in your body floating and unfloating there.

When you can float away from the wall, your front float may look like this:

Front float, at ease. Notice how relaxed her head, back, and arms look. Is that you? You don't have to hold your knees straight like this, though. That's work.

UNFLOATING WHILE AWAY FROM THE WALL

When you're front-floating some distance from the wall, you can use your abdominal muscles to draw your knees under you and place your feet on the bottom of the pool directly under your face. You may have already done this at the wall.

As you draw your knees under you, you may also use your hands to help you unfloat. With your hands dangling naturally, lift them gently toward the surface so that they're ahead of your shoulders. With your flat palms and the undersides of your arms, push downward on the water. This, along with using your abdominals, will bring your knees up and forward so you can then place your feet on the bottom. Remain in control and quiet inside. Once your feet are on the bottom, you can lift your head out.

When you can unfloat in the middle of the pool, you will have reached a milestone: freedom from the wall! When you reach this point, know that a world of your learn-to-swim comrades stands to applaud you!

GIVE YOURSELF A STANDING OVATION

No kidding. You've experienced a truth about water that you've always wanted to know. The water holds you up (unless you're one of the few who sink), and now you're in control enough to stand up when you want to.

TRAP

If, while you're practicing a front float, you're thinking, "I wonder if this will work in the deep end," you're falling into a trap. Your body is in the shallow end, but *you're in the deep end*.

If you're in the deep end while your body is in the shallow end, you're out of your body. Therefore, your practice in the shallow will not be fruitful. You won't be able to feel every aspect of the float—for example, that the water is holding you up, or that you have tension in your limbs or neck, or that you have X amount of air, etc. What's more, you'll miss the realization that by doing nothing, the water supports you. If unfloating doesn't work well, or if you're in a hurry while you do it, check to see if you're in the deep end while your body is in the shallow.

2+2=4
YOU HAVE TO BE IN YOUR BODY TO KNOW WHAT YOU'RE FEELING.

Once you can feel all that the water is doing for you, you can notice what's left for you to do—if anything.

FEELING AS THOUGH YOU'LL FLIP OVER

Sometimes, as people go into their front float the first few times, they have the sensation that they will flip all the way over, as in a somersault.

You may or may not believe it, but it's absolutely impossible for you to flip over, head over heels. Many students say that when they begin to feel their feet rising up behind them, it feels as though the feet will just continue to rise. But they can't rise above the water's surface. And there's nothing to make your head go down. The buoyancy of your head is more powerful than gravity's force on it.

I am not asking you to bite off more than you can chew with this feeling of flipping. If you feel as though you may flip over, you'll need to control your float. Hold onto something. When your feet begin to float to the surface and it starts to feel scary, come out of the float and stand up. Stay in your body. Remember:

WE DON'T CARE IF YOU FLOAT
WE ONLY CARE THAT YOU REMAIN IN CONTROL

Take time to experience the water holding you up, mid-pool. Give yourself days to practice this.

I have to say that when I finally felt the water support me and I could let go, I felt an extraordinary ease traveling through the water. I realized how inefficient it was for me to have expended so much energy and worry, keeping myself above water...when the water can do that for me. Slowing down and trusting the water to support me was counterintuitive for me.

—Melonie

FEELING WOBBLY

If you're floating and you feel wobbly, it's probably because you're holding your head up too high. Can you feel your neck working? The more you allow your body and head to be supported by the water, the more stable you'll be.

I don't mean you have to stick your head down further into the water than it naturally goes when you rest it. If the wobbly feeling doesn't disappear when you let your head rest in the water, then you're probably holding your feet or hands up.

Can you feel your muscles tensing? If so, allow yourself to feel all the work you're doing. When you allow yourself all that work, you're likely to have the thought, "Why am I working so hard?" When you stop, the wobbling will stop.

BEING A SINKER

Are you a true sinker? In shoulder-deep water, if you hold onto the wall, take a maximum breath, and dangle in the water and you find yourself with your head below the surface and your knees parked on the bottom in four or five feet of water (five feet, if you're tall), you're probably a sinker. A sinker is a person who, when he fills his lungs maximally and then lies face down on the water, goes to the bottom and doesn't float back to the surface. Try it again with the biggest breath you can hold. If you drop to the bottom, you are a sinker.

Congratulations! Being a sinker is being one of the few. You might look upon sinking with a sinking feeling. You're entitled to this, but it's not necessary. Virtually every male swimmer and many female swimmers on every Olympic swim team in the world are sinkers. But they're good swimmers, aren't they? Are they confident and comfortable in deep water? We hope so. Furthermore, every male Olympic *athlete* and all the women marathon runners, sprinters, pentathletes, and others with very lean bodies are likely sinkers as well. There's no reason for this to be an emergency. It's possible for you to sink and sit on the bottom, smiling. You simply need to be in your body when you sink.

Just because you sink does not mean that you won't be able to keep yourself at the surface when you want to, in any position that anyone else can float in. You'll just need to learn how. While swimming, you'll stay afloat with the speed you derive from propelling yourself; you won't have to do extra work to stay afloat.

I'm not saying you have to swim fast to stay up; you don't. When you stop swimming, you'll need to apply just a little effort, doing something efficient. But the effort requires no inner hurry.

If you're a sinker, take time to practice what naturally happens when you give your body over to the combined effects of water and gravity. Take a big breath. In shallow water, drop forward onto the surface. Let yourself keep dropping down to the bottom and then kneel, sit or lie there. Is it okay with you to park on the bottom? After you've done that a few times, you may want to try turning onto your side as though you were watching TV on your bed, head propped on hand.

All he needs is a TV.

If you either hold your nose or wear a nose clip you can also lie on your back. This is something very, very few people can do or have ever done. Count yourself among the elite.

Are you getting any sense of how important it is, and what a difference it makes, to be in control? If, as you read, you're following the steps of each lesson but you're not making *staying in control* and *staying comfortable* the first priority, the struggle will continue. You're relearning how to learn. It's easier to slow down and have fun. You will learn to swim *if* you're comfortable.

ONCE YOU'RE IN CONTROL, YOU CAN SWIM,
SHALLOW AND DEEP.

STEP 36: PRACTICE WHILE YOU'RE CALM

Be gentle and kind to yourself. You're doing a good job of learning, of making the proper thing your first priority (staying comfortable). Are you seeing things in a new light? You aren't going too slowly, even if you think you are.

Give yourself plenty of time. Stay true to yourself and don't allow yourself to hurry. Getting the basics down now will make a huge difference to you later. It pays to go slowly. If you unfloat in a hurry, you may find yourself standing up with only one foot on the ground or falling forward and having to regain your balance. Do it more slowly next time. Stay comfortable.

Unfloating is not important; comfort is. This is the purpose of unfloating with the rail or wall there. Start with lots of air and go *slowly*. You want to learn to be comfortable. So, practice comfort.

Practice the unfloat—or anything—forty or fifty times. It's not the number of repetitions that counts; it's your full presence that counts. Practice as long as you're having fun. There won't be any question in your mind when you've got it down. If there is, you don't.

Catching yourself
As you learn to stay in your body, first you learn to catch yourself leaving.
Then you learn to prevent yourself from leaving altogether.

STEP 37: REVIEW

Over the course of your practice, it pays to do the following each time:
- Hold onto the wall
- Take a breath
- Let your body dangle in the water with no support from your hands or arms even though you're holding on
- Feel the water hold you up
- When you have the thoughts, "My hands aren't holding me up. My feet aren't holding me up. The water is. Maybe I don't need my hands on the wall anymore," you'll probably let your hands slide off the gutter.
- Then, while you still have plenty of air, unfloat.

If you know you'll be safe, you'll be able to let go of the wall without leaving the 1st Circle: mission accomplished.

STEP 38: WHICH WAY IS THE RIGHT WAY?

Often students say, "Did I do it right?" And I say, "Did you accomplish your goal?"

If they say, "Yes," then they did it right. Doing a skill at this tender stage of learning is all about *whether it's comfortable*. If it's comfortable, it's right. If it makes you happy, it's right. If it functions, the form is good enough for now.

If a skill stops working—that is, if you notice something uncomfortable that you didn't notice before—something needs to change. It may have felt good before, but only in comparison to how bad the previous attempts felt! When you find a way that isn't comfortable, the new goal is to make it so. Reaching that goal will improve your skill. That becomes the new "right."

STEP 39: FEEL THE WATER HOLD YOU UP ON YOUR BACK

Ideally, you'll have shallow water—two feet or less—to learn the back float. If not, you can use any pool that has gutters or a lip to hold onto. First, we'll go through the steps of learning in two feet or less water. If you don't have water this shallow to learn in, skip down to the next step, "Learning the Back Float at the Wall."

Sit down on the pool floor in very shallow water. One or two feet of depth will work. The more buoyant you are, the shallower it can be, down to about 8 inches. Place your hands a little bit behind you on the bottom.

Sit down in very shallow water with your hands behind you.

Start with your heels on the bottom and let them stay there. If they float up on their own, it's okay. Lie back until your head and ears are in the water. Keep your hands on the bottom. Take a breath and hold it. Do you feel the water supporting you?

Lie back until your head and ears are in the water.

Begin a back float in very shallow water; once you feel the water supporting you, you can slowly lift your hands. These people feel the float.

If you do, then if you feel safe, allow your hands to barely rise off the bottom and continue to feel yourself held by the water. Floating means letting the water hold you up with no movement on your part. Spend lots of time feeling the water hold you up on your back.

Using a Tether for the Back Float

Connect the short strap to the pole, ladder, hook, or Float Bar—your mooring.

Hold onto the mooring with both hands. You may have to straddle a pole. Holding on is the best way to feel the water hold you up. Don't hold on with only one hand: your attention will be on that hand, not the feeling of floating.

Spend an hour over several days feeling the water hold you up on your back, holding on. Notice if breathing affects your "altitude." This will show you how you keep your nose and mouth above the surface without effort.

When you're convinced that the water is holding you up, let your hands down into the water. The tether will keep you close. Pull on it to return to the mooring. By doing this many times, as long as you feel comfortable, you will make up a way to unfloat by yourself.

Hold on and come up at your leisure.

After he felt safe, he added the middle strap and floated further away.

V FLOAT, MID-POOL

If you find your seat dropping or your face sinking below the surface, you may notice that you're trying to hold your feet off the bottom. This will not work. If your feet seem to want to stay on the bottom despite you, let them stay. If they float by themselves, let them. Don't try to hold them up. You may be a person who floats with his feet on the bottom, especially in water this shallow.

V Float: a mistake
The V float results from trying to hold your feet up.
Your belief pulls your face under; "I should be
horizontal, so, I must hold my feet up."

Troubleshooting a V Float

When you lie back to float on your back, go ahead and let yourself lift your feet off the bottom again on purpose. In other words, let yourself do the very thing that pulls you under—the thing that doesn't work. You may as well let yourself do it, because you weren't in control of *doing it* before and it's likely that you're not in control of *not* doing it now. (This is not meant to be a challenge. I could be wrong if you've changed something.) ♡

If your nose is going under water, use a nose clip or hold your nose. By consciously letting yourself do that which comes naturally—i.e. the V float, even though it isn't the back float—and doing it several times, you'll begin to get some control over it. You'll discover how you were using your abs to lift your feet, causing your face to go under. You'll see how you caused yourself to "sink." If you let your feet fall, your float will work. Now, you'll have control over it.

2+2=4
TO GET CONTROL OVER SOMETHING THAT ISN'T WORKING, DO IT INCORRECTLY ON PURPOSE.

**In a back float, allow your feet to fall.
Now he's got it. No more V float.**

Now, I presume that you're floating comfortably. After you have lain on your back in a float for a few seconds, you may wish to start breathing. You'll notice the effect that your breathing has on your position. When you breathe out, you drop a bit. If you breathe out too much, you might sink below the surface. You'll probably put your hands on the bottom before this happens. When you breathe in, you rise up. As you have learned, the amount of air you have affects your position.

To remain afloat, some people need to keep a certain amount of air in their lungs and not exhale more than that amount. This doesn't mean you have to hold your breath; you just can't let out *all* of it. Find if you need to breathe shallowly in order to maintain buoyancy for a comfortable float.

Some very buoyant people can exhale all their air and still remain afloat. Many people wish they were buoyant enough to do this. Some people have to hold a maximal breath in order to float. These are the near-sinkers. Some people sink even if they hold the maximum possible amount of air in their lungs. These are the sinkers. We'll address this situation again later.

Practice the back float for fun. Once you feel quite comfortable in your back float, experiment with the position of your hands. When lying on your back in a float, you can put your hands wherever they feel most comfortable. NOTE: if you take your hands out of the water, the weight of them above the surface will push you under water. They cannot float if they're in the air.

Experiment with putting your hands straight out to the sides at 3:00 and 9:00, as you picture a clock: your head is at 12:00 and your feet are at 6:00. Does your body position change?

Buoyancy and back float

STEP 40: LEARNING THE BACK FLOAT AT THE WALL

If you're using a pool that has a gutter or edge you can hold onto, you can learn the back float at the wall. Don't try to learn the back float without holding onto something—the wall, a ladder, or the bottom of the pool—unless you can stay in your body for it.

- In three to five feet of water, face the wall and hold the gutter/wall with both hands.
- Place your body flush against the wall so that your chest, stomach and thighs are all touching the wall. Your hands will be supporting your weight and your knees will be bent, the tops of your feet resting on the bottom (see below).
- Lower yourself so that your chin is almost resting in the water. Don't support yourself with your feet on the bottom; support yourself with your hands.

Steps of the back float at the wall:

Whole front surface except shins touching wall. Feet rest on the bottom but they don't support you.

Then, this:

Lie back as though your head were on your pillow.

Not this:

Slowly lie back in the water by extending your arms. Let your ears go into the water and let your head rest in the water as though it were on your pillow. Your head will be away from the wall a foot or two, and your hands will still be on the wall. Don't let go of the wall. In this position, get the feeling of lying back on the water as though it were a mattress.

Then, notice whether it's your hands holding you up, your feet, or the water holding you up.

If you're not comfortable putting your ears in, go back to the section on making it comfortable. We (you and I) don't want you to be uncomfortable at any time.

The object is to remain in the 1st Circle at all times.

See if you can allow yourself to be supported by the water alone. Let the water do all the work. Your hands will be on the wall preventing you from floating away. But they won't support your weight.

Take a breath and hold it.

What happens? Can you feel your body rise? If you can't feel the water holding you up, take a bigger breath and hold it when you lie down on the water. You won't be letting go of the wall at any time, so you don't have to worry. Make sure you're not holding yourself out of the water with your arms.

Most students can feel the water holding them up. If you don't, make sure you have the correct body position at the wall. (See photos above, "Then this" and "Not this.")

Come to know the feeling of being supported by the water, with no effort on your part. Give yourself time to find comfort and certainty. If you can't feel the water holding you up, and you're in the correct position, then it's possible that your body is too dense to float. If you have a lot of muscle and bone relative to your total body weight, you may be denser than water and a sinker. You're still a born swimmer. Remember what we said about Olympians. Later, we'll address how to stay afloat if you're a sinker.

TROUBLESHOOTING A BACK FLOAT AT THE WALL

If you don't stay afloat on your back, add one detail: take the biggest breath you possibly can. Hold it until you're ready to unfloat. If you're sure you'll go under water, use a nose clip to prevent water in your nose.

STEP 41: UNFLOATING FROM A BACK FLOAT

While you're holding onto the wall, obviously, you can unfloat easily by pulling yourself up. When you're convinced that the water holds you up, there comes a time when you're likely to be curious about letting go. Remember, it's more important to remain in control than to let go of the wall. If you know you can remain in control if you float away from the wall, go ahead.

If you're not sure you can remain in control, don't let go. If you did, you'd be practicing being out the 1st Circle.

If you know you can remain in control when letting go of the wall, go into your back float at the wall. When the water is holding you up and you feel safe, let go of the wall and allow yourself to drift a foot or two away. To unfloat, take a breath and curl up, tucking your chin and drawing your knees toward your head. By pulling your knees and head together, your body will automatically rotate forward into a position where you can simply put your feet down on the bottom. It may seem counterintuitive to pull your feet up to put them down, but this is the way it works. It works well. Your face will go under water. The key is to do it slowly, staying in the 1st Circle. You have enough air.

Steps to unfloat from a back float.
If you're a horizontal floater, the figure on the left would be horizontal.

If you wish, you can also push upward on the water with your flat palms and forearms as your arms come forward, as the swimmer does above. She started by putting her hands at 3:00 and 9:00.

Give yourself permission to put your face in the water for a couple of seconds while your body is rotating into position to put your feet down. Is it okay for your face to go in? If not, then return to the section on putting your face in. You would not want to skip this step or to force your face to do something you don't like. This would put you in the 2nd or 3rd Circle. Stay in the 1st Circle all the time.

If you're not sure you can remain in control when you let go of the wall, move to a ladder. Someone else who wishes to use the ladder at any point has the right of way, of course. Stand so that your side is close to the ladder. Lie back in a back float with one hand on the vertical rail of the ladder and the other hand free. The hand on the ladder should be holding on below the surface. This way, your hand will be closer to its natural floating position.

See if you can feel the water holding you up. See if you can feel it holding you up with your hand behind the ladder but touching it. Use the ladder to unfloat if you want it.

Then see if you can unfloat with your hand behind the ladder and the security of knowing it's there if you need it. If there is any tension in your body, stop and feel it. If it makes you nervous to let go of the ladder, it's not time to do it yet. Perhaps you aren't sure that the water is doing all the work. Return to that.

Practice the unfloat until you own it. As you know, this is another big milestone that frees you. Give yourself *hours* of practice to learn it. It may not take that long, but give yourself that long.

TRYING TO GET YOUR FEET OFF THE BOTTOM

When I say, "It's okay to let your feet stay on the bottom," students often don't believe me. They have a deep belief that floating means that their feet will be off the bottom. They think that if their feet are on the bottom in the shallow end, they'll also be on the bottom in the deep end.

The next photo shows what actually happens. This student who floats with her feet on the bottom in shallow water floats very well in the deep end. Her feet hang down, but they don't reach the bottom. The buoyancy of her upper body is enough for her whole body to float.

Students ask, "Shouldn't I practice floating with my feet off the bottom in shallow water so that when I get to the deep, I'll be able to do it correctly?" *No.* When you're in shallow water, find your natural float in shallow water. When you're in deep water, find your natural float in deep water. If you're thinking about deep water while you're in shallow water, your body is in shallow water and *you're* in deep water. You won't be able to feel the back float and therefore, you won't learn it.

If your feet sink in shallow water, then in deep water, you'll probably look like this. This is a back float in deep water for someone whose feet don't float. A perfectly good back float.

Another pitfall of trying too hard in a back float is trying to kick both your feet up. You'd most likely end up in a V float again.

Do you ever find yourself doing this?

Trying to lift one foot off the bottom.

What would happen if you allowed your feet to stay on the bottom and let the water do all the work?

If you allow your feet to drop, they may park on the bottom, like this. If you kick them up, they'll end up like this every time... back on the bottom. This is a perfectly good back float.

You'd feel an easy back float for the first time. If your feet are meant to float up, they will on their own. Otherwise, they'll stay down where they belong for your body type.

Trap

Remember not to fall into this trap: "My body is in the shallow end, but *I'm* in the deep end."

Arm Positions in the Back Float

I recommend wearing a nose clip for this next lesson. Experiment with having your hands at 10:00 and 2:00. Then try 11:00 and 1:00. Do you notice how your floating position changes? You're feeling the seesaw effect of redistributing your weight so that your body levels off: with your arms overhead at 12:00, more weight is at your upper end. Your feet may come off the bottom.

Arms at almost 10:00 and 2:00.

Arms at 6:00.

What happens if you put your hands at 12:00 (keeping them below the surface)?

Arms at 12:00: notice how she became more horizontal compared to the previous photo.

NOTE: Some people don't have enough flexibility in their shoulders to put their arms at 12:00 without having their arms come slightly out of the water. Remember, if your arms come out of the water, you're likely to go under. If you can't put your arms at 12:00, put them as close to 12:00 as you can, to float most horizontally.

You can also experiment with arm positions in your front float. When you float on your front, where do your arms naturally go without effort? Most people think they're supposed to hold their arms straight out front to float correctly. (That type of float is more like a prone float.) However, a front float is a state of being held up with no effort on your part; don't hold your arms up. If you let your arms (and legs) go where gravity—and buoyancy—take them, you'll find your natural front float.

2+2=4

WATER IS A DIFFERENT ENVIRONMENT. YOU CAN'T
LEARN TO SWIM AS THOUGH IT WEREN'T THERE.
YOU NEED TO FEEL IT.

STEP 42: EXPERIMENT WITH YOUR BACK FLOAT AFTER YOU OWN IT

Lie on your back in the shallow end. How do you feel? If there's any tension in your body, allow it to be there. As you let it be there, your body will let it go if your nose is safe. You'll come back into your body.

Did you try it? What happened?

Can you play in your back float? If so, play with the position of your limbs one at a time and see how your balance changes. Use a nose clip. What makes you roll over onto your front? What makes you go under? What makes you stay on your back? What makes you float higher? Is there anything you can do to sink (go to the bottom) on purpose? I doubt it!

REVIEW

Many people float with their feet on the bottom in the shallow end. Why fight it? If they were in deep water, their feet wouldn't reach the bottom. But in the shallow end, their feet drop because their legs are denser than the water. It's okay. They don't want to waste their energy trying to keep their feet off the bottom when the water keeps their bodies afloat all by itself. Why would you?

PRACTICE

Over a few days, spend time floating on your back. Just lie there, as though you were on your bed.

Then, dangle on your stomach, hanging in the water like a wet noodle. In both floats, let gravity have your limbs and head. See what it feels like to do absolutely nothing except hold a comfortable breath.

You need to be at ease doing nothing before you can be at ease doing something. Play with doing nothing.

FIVE GOOD BACK FLOATS

Each of these floats is perfectly good. There's nothing missing from any of them.

There are many more good back floats, too.

Each of the floats above is perfectly good. The fourth floater has her wrists cocked. Her float would be fine, too, if she didn't cock her wrists. She cocked them to make her hands vertical which makes them rise above the surface. This puts downward force at the upper end of her body, causing her legs to rise so she floats more horizontally. She also tucked her feet under her to bring more of her weight toward the center of her body. Not that you should or must float horizontally. This is simply an option to experiment with, to find out how things work.

Step 43: Games and Toys That Teach

Games and toys are fun experiences we contrive in the water to learn how the water works. A toy in this case is a movement you can play with.

Sitting on the Bottom

See if you can sit on the bottom of the pool in water that's 3-5 feet deep. Only do this if it sounds like fun, of course! The game is to park your suit on the bottom of the pool (without taking your suit off)! Bouncing off the bottom is an intermediate step toward parking, but it's not the goal. See if you can sit down and stay for 3-4 seconds.

Parked and proud

Sitting on the bottom takes more know-how than you may have thought. How can the student above sit on the bottom and not panic? He knows he's safe. He has learned to be in control in water; he's getting to know it. There was a time when sitting on the bottom of a pool was the last thing on his agenda. He may have thought it was a crazy idea at first, but he was curious. Since he wanted to get there, he was in his body—he could receive signals his body was giving him, and he could keep himself safe. Eventually he figured out how to remain in complete control and to sink on purpose. Now he can't think of a reason to panic.

What would it take for you to lose your buoyancy and sink? The process of learning to swim should include learning how hard it is to sink. Learning to sink helps teach you how the water and your body work together. It's worthwhile!

If you can sit on the bottom, you may want to try lying down, too.

A novel feeling

Lying on your back on the bottom is novel. As previously mentioned, use a nose clip, or hold your nose. The goal of this game is not really to sit or lie on the bottom; it's to find out how hard it is to get there. It's to understand that in order to sink, you really need to know how to do it. If you don't know how, you won't sink, if you are not a sinker. The only way a person can sink if they are normally buoyant is if they panic and exhaust themselves by thrashing and giving up all their air. Even then, they may not sink.

When you have an experience that takes your body to a new "place," you can expect that in the next few days you'll have a brand new thought. It may not have anything to do with swimming. But because you went into new territory with a new physical experience, you can expect to go into new territory mentally soon after.

BECOMING A BALL

After you feel quite confident in your front float, draw yourself from a front float into a smaller package. Contract your body so that you're no longer a body length long, but a foot shorter, pulling your knees toward your head. As you know, we don't care if you move in the direction of making a ball; we *only* care that you feel in control as you move.

Front float away from wall:

When you've been in this new position for a while and you're quite at home with it, contract a little more. Pull your arms and feet closer together so that you're nearer to the shape of a ball. Again, we don't care if you move toward being in a ball; only that you feel in control as you go.

Making your body into a smaller package on your way to becoming a ball.

If, as you move toward being in a ball you start to leave the 1st Circle, go back to a more extended position to return to the 1st Circle. Wait in this position until your body gives you signals that it's safe to proceed.

If you're in control and it sounds like fun, pull yourself fully into a ball, with your arms wrapped around your knees.

The ball

Notice how your balance changes just a little bit when you're in a ball. Stand up whenever you want.

Go back into the ball and rest there. Get to know "ball." You can't hang suspended like this on land. Enjoy it!

Why is this important to swimming? Because it teaches you something about your balance in water. Because it helps you to understand how your body and the water work together. Because you're practicing being present (in control). Because it brings your awareness and presence to a new position. Because each new position you reach teaches you that you can do one more thing in water that makes you that much freer. If you're like my students, you want to be able to play.

BOUNCING BALL

If there's a friend in the pool with you, you can take turns being a ball or being a bouncer. When you're the ball, your friend can place his hands on your back and gently push you toward the bottom. It should be a gentle push so that you don't reach the bottom with your toes. Then, just wait. In 3 to 4 seconds, your body will stop going toward the bottom (at the effect of his push) and will start to float back up at the effect of your buoyancy.

You'll bob back up to the surface. Your balance will change a bit. Then, if you have plenty of air and you stay in the ball position, your friend can push you back down again. It's just another playful thing you can do in water that you can't do on land that teaches you how the water works.

When Joan was the ball (and was having a ball), her knees grazed the bottom from this slightly too enthusiastic push.

SMILING UNDER WATER

Go under water and see if you can smile. You could smile a toothy smile, or a closed-mouth smile. When you feel safe, you'll find the toothy smile rewarding.

Next, try coughing under water. Then pretend you're sneezing. Naturally, you would only do the exhaling part of both coughing and sneezing. You can also swallow under water with your mouth closed. It's good to know that if you need to do any of these things, you can be safe.

DANGLE

Hang in a front float. Imagine that you can attach a Relaxation Meter to your entire body. On a scale from 1-100, (100 being totally limp), what would it

155

read? If it doesn't read 100, dangle again. Feel your shoulders, back, neck, arms, legs, abdomen, jaw, ankles, fingers. Feel any tension you find and let it be there. Don't try to change it. What does your body do when you don't resist it?

PERMISSION TO USE NOSE CLIPS

From this point forward, if you haven't already agreed to one, I highly recommend that you use a nose clip. Though you can learn to prevent water from going into your nose as we discussed before, and you can hold your nose, if you have not mastered keeping water out of your nose yet and you try a new skill without a nose clip, you'll be splitting your attention between the new skill and keeping water out of your nose. This, we have established, does not work.

Resist any temptation to think you "should" know how to keep water out of your nose. Let yourself be where you are. This helps you to come back to your body where you can learn.

The next lesson is one that will require that you protect your nose. Therefore, please get a nose clip if you haven't already.

PHOTOS IN THE MIDST OF LEARNING

Here are a few photos of students who had taken most of the steps in this book; they started from where you are now, or close.

You learn so well when you're having fun. But first, you need to feel safe. These people became safe.

Picture yourself having fun in the pool. What would your photo look like?

> *We stopped to witness the miracle of classmates floating freely and joyfully for the first time after years or even decades of terror in the water. For most of us, whether we were young adults, middle-aged, or elderly, it was the first time we experienced childlike glee and freedom in the water.*
>
> *When every cell of our being was finally convinced the water would hold us up, we floated and paddled around in the deep end of the pool. And when it happened, it felt miraculous and completely natural and thrilling and transformational. And we did it without learning the crawl stroke, the flutter kick or the butterfly. We did it by going slowly, step by step, until we internalized confidence and trust in the water. Not one of us believed Melon in the beginning when she said each of us was born a swimmer the same way she was born a swimmer. Now we knew it was true.*
>
> —Tut, *"A Novel Approach to Healing Fear of the Water"*

STEP 44: STEERING

Each time you get into the water, start at the beginning. Review the basics and become quiet inside. Remember, it rarely works to try to pick up where you left off last time when you're learning to swim.

In the water when you're ready, go back into a ball. Review "ball" for awhile. Then, let go of your knees with one hand. How does your balance feel? If you're comfortable, use the flat palm of one hand to push on the water so that you turn sideways 360 degrees (a complete circle, called a "360"). Maybe you have enough air to turn several circles. If it sounds like fun, turn the other direction using the same hand.

Turn counterclockwise: if you push right on the water, you'll move to the left.
Turn clockwise: if you push left on the water, you'll move to the right.

Then, use your other hand and turn a 360. When you're familiar with the way that feels, use that same hand to turn a 360 in the other direction. Then, use both hands to turn a 360. How can you use your hands in such a way that they *both* help you turn in the direction you want to go? Play. Goof around.

STEP 45: FIND HAND POSITIONS THAT WORK

Go into your ball again and turn yourself in a 360. This time, experiment with different hand positions. First, turn a 360 with your fist clenched (just one hand). Notice the purchase (the grip, traction, amount of pressure) you get on the water with your hand in a fist. How well does it propel you, relative to the effort you use?

Next, do a 360 with your hand open, fingers splayed. How does this feel compared to the efficiency of your fist?

Fingers splayed

Next, do a 360 with your hand cupped.

Hand cupped. How does this efficiency compare?

Next, do a 360 with your hand horizontal, so you push on the water with the edge of your hand. How well does this work?

When you're rested, try a 360 with your hand flat, like a pancake, so you're pushing with your whole palm and the face of your fingers, which are together. It's okay if your thumb is away from your palm. To have it touching your palm takes more effort than it's worth.

Both hands are flat as a pancake. "Pancake hands."
Both the palms and the backs of your hands are as flat as a pancake.

How well does this hand position work compared to the others? Swimming students have been told for decades that the correct hand position for maximum efficiency is cupped. Perhaps you could tell that other positions allowed you to move more effectively in your 360. If so, you know that cupped hands are not efficient. You might have intuited that cupped hands were not correct, as it's too much work. If something is a lot of work in the water, chances are that it's not correct. Something simpler and easier works better.

Other hand positions also demand too much work for the same amount of movement. Therefore, they are not used in swimming. The most efficient position, and perhaps you found it for yourself, is the last one: flat as a pancake. Make this efficient hand position a habit.

STEP 46: FEEL, DON'T THINK

While you're learning, it's fine to focus on the most workable hand position. But focus on the *feeling* of it. Look at your hand and feel what works best for you. Do it over and over until it becomes second nature. Don't try to add to this skill until you have embodied it.

Why feel instead of think? Because when you feel, you increase your presence—in this case, in your hand. Your hand gives you feedback to let you know what's happening. You will recognize an efficient position as opposed to an inefficient one.

You also would want to feel instead of thinking because you don't want to try to remember how to hold your hand at the same time that you try to remember the step that builds on hand position. You can't have your attention in two places at once. As we said earlier, if you try, you're not fully present to either one. Therefore, you can't learn either one.

Sometimes I see someone swimming with his hands in a strange position. I know that he didn't learn by feeling. He was thinking more than feeling when this position was "learned." He never would have said, "This feels right." As a result, he didn't learn the efficient way. He is now swimming slower and working harder than necessary.

Be completely in your body for the one thing you're doing. Practice it until it comes naturally. When you can do it "on automatic," you've mastered it enough to do it without being fully present. When you've mastered it enough to do it without being fully present, you'll have attention to spare for learning something else. Only then is it time to learn something new.

I know you know this. But how often in our lives do we ignore this truth and try to cram more into our time than it's possible to absorb? It doesn't work. Give yourself the best chance to succeed by setting up the situation to work every time. Give yourself time to play and absorb each lesson into your body.

WHAT IS SWIMMING, TO YOU?

What does it mean to know how to swim? Does it mean doing the freestyle, fast and pretty? Is it getting from here to there, no matter how uncomfortable it feels? Or, is it moving and stopping easily and confidently without regard to depth?

As mentioned earlier, I define knowing how to swim as confidence in water over your head. Once you're confident in shallow water, you'll automatically be able to move from here to there (swim) with comfort and ease. It's the comfort and ease that makes it swimming! Without comfort and ease, it's merely stroking. Once you're confident in deep water, you'll be able to swim in deep water with comfort and ease. Once you've learned how to do that—to *swim*—you can then learn to swim *efficiently*. Strokes are the key to swimming efficiently. Conventional lessons tried to teach you to swim *efficiently* before you learned to swim. It didn't work. Now you're on the right path: comfort comes first.

EASE

What is it that makes you feel at ease in the water?

For most people, it's having enough air, knowing they can remain in control, and being able to rest when they want to. Anyone who's worried about sinking is only worried because he isn't in control of coming back up for air. Is this true for you? Ease comes from knowing you're in control.

From time to time I find myself sinking without planning to. It's usually when I'm in the deep end under water watching students. It happens because I took a smaller breath than I needed in order to stay in place. It's a humorous moment when I find myself not staying at the level where I'd planned to be. But why worry? I'm in control. By pushing down on the water, I come right back up. – Melon

Step 47: Propulsion, Your First Swim

Ease is the operative word, whether you're swimming in the shallow or deep. Hopefully, you wouldn't "put yourself out" (to the 2nd or 3rd Circle) to swim. Your goal is to be in your body.

If you haven't moved from here to there in the water yet with ease, try this in shallow water. Lying in a front float, hang there listlessly. Feel how the water holds you up. You don't have to hold yourself up, right? The water does all the work. You're not kicking your feet off the bottom, are you? If you are, you haven't learned the front float yet and it's *not* time to swim. Be kind to yourself and return to the section on front float.

If you want to move from here to there, you don't have to do anything to stay up; you only have to do something to take yourself over there.

Starting Position

Start in a front float.

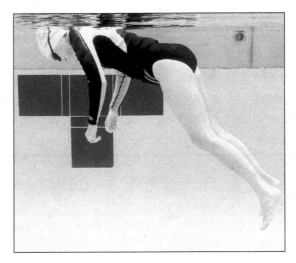

Front float

Spend a few minutes in one position. You'll be looking at the bottom of the pool and slightly backward, not forward. Dangle listlessly.

TIPPING: REMINDER

If you feel yourself tipping, you're probably holding your head up. Let it rest in the water. Sometimes tipping is caused by tension. Can you feel any? Let it be there. If that isn't the problem, then another way to stabilize is to spread your hands apart. If you need more stability, you can spread your feet apart as well. Experiment. When you're comfortable, you're ready to continue.

ARM PULL

With both arms outstretched directly in front of you, pull your flat pancake hands backward to your thighs. Do this by pressing on the water with the palms of your hands and the entire inside surface of your arms. In other words, form the largest surface area you can with your hands and arms in order to push on the greatest amount of water. Flat hands create the largest surface.

This is the correct hand position for stroking. He pulls himself through the water efficiently.

After you've swept your hands and arms back to your thighs, leave them there. Let yourself glide through the water as far as your sweep takes you. Why not get all the distance that's possible? That way it takes fewer strokes to go from here to there, therefore using less energy. Most people can glide longer than they think they can.

Spend time at the end of your arm sweep, coasting. Keep coasting even if your feet drop. The whole time, you're looking straight down at the bottom.

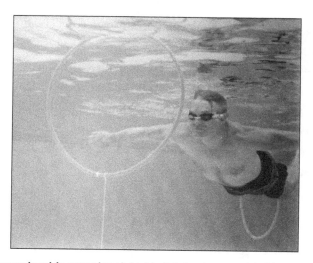

Sweeping his arms back to his thighs, he propels himself...

...through the hoop.

After your arm sweep, when your forward motion dies down, bring your hands back to the front, creating the smallest amount of resistance possible. Draw them from your sides together under your belly, one atop the other. With the palms of your hands almost touching your belly, slide your hands up your torso, the thumbs and edges of your hands slicing through the water, all the way up until your hands are out in front of you again. Turn your hands over as you reach forward at the end of this recovery (recovery is the return to the beginning of the arm sweep). Recovering efficiently prevents you from creating excess drag.

When your hands are out in front of you again, take another arm sweep back to your sides with your "pancake" palms and inner arms. Feel the pressure on the flat palms of your hands and insides of your arms all the way through your sweep. Your *palms are the most important part* of your body in propelling you through the water. Put your attention in your (pancake) palms. By taking strokes, you'll go from here to there. Let your legs trail quietly.

TRAP

When you begin to swim from here to there, you may be tempted to see if you can swim *all the way* across, or to see *how far* you can go. This is the "get to the side rather than enjoy the trip" trap. If you're focused on getting to a certain point, you won't feel what you're doing; *you'll be* at that point. Remember, the goal is to stay where your body is.

Start swimming again, but this time, and forevermore, be where your body is while you propel yourself. Feel the sweep with your palms. Feel yourself moving through the water. Watch the bottom go by. Feel the glide. Feel your air supply. By being in your body, you'll know what to do in each moment to keep yourself comfortable. Your body will tell you, and you'll be there to hear it.

Congratulations for understanding this distinction and using it.

You are entering swimmerhood.

THE MOST IMPORTANT FACTORS IN LEARNING TO SWIM

What are the most important things to learn about swimming? Would you say,

"Not drowning"?

"Staying up"?

"Getting to the other side"?

"Being able to breathe"?

I believe the most important things to learn are these, in this order:
- Fun

- Permission

- Comfort

- Control

These all boil down to one thing: fun.

PERMISSION

It's okay to be yourself, to go slowly, to experiment, ask all your questions and say "no, thanks." You are the person to give yourself this permission. It means, "I don't need to push myself." It's the first step of optimal success.

FUN AND COMFORT

Fun and comfort are mandatory from my point of view. They are not only the whole point, they are non-negotiable for learning happily the first time, every time. They all but guarantee learning.

CONTROL

We've already established that without control, you can't get anything else done. Control is a number one priority. Control means presence of mind. You are "here."

BREATHING

Yes, breathing is important. However, your breath isn't accessible unless you're in control. Once you're in control and having fun, you can learn it all.

IMPISH TEMPTATION

Let's say you're able to swim a few strokes across the pool with the arm sweep and glide. As you swim along and it's working well, you have the thought, "I can do this. Now, how do I take a breath?" You start trying to get a breath.

It's very likely that if you've only swum a few strokes across the pool a few times, you are not 100% in your body yet. You aren't 100% in control of yourself. But the temptation to try the next step is often great. To ask yourself to be in control of getting a breath at this point is *not reasonable*.

How *does* it work, then? In order to get a breath, you must not be attached to whether or not you get one. But the impish thought is likely to be rife with attachment: "If I could *only* get a breath!"

If you try to learn to breathe at this point in the game, it is likely to place you "on hold" (stuck, contracted about breathing) for weeks, months, or even years. I don't want to put any limitations on you, but it's highly unlikely that it's time for you to try to get a breath right now (except if you stand up to get one) unless you're completely in the 1st Circle. I urge you not to. Spend more time just pulling and gliding, feeling everything and enjoying it.

Instead of trying to get a breath, go back a step. Spend more time—lots more time—swimming along with your arm sweeps, gliding, learning. Learn about your glide time. Learn about your balance and how it shifts. Learn where your feet are throughout your glide. Learn about the position of your hands as you sweep. How few strokes can you use to go a certain distance? What position is your head in? What are you looking at? How long does your air last? Are you having fun?

You must be completely in control to learn to swim. You must be completely in control swimming before you can learn to breathe while swimming.

GOING BACKWARD IS GOING FORWARD

Jerry came to class to learn to breathe. He did not believe that he was afraid in water. He had taken swimming lessons and had many swimming skills, but he had not been able to learn to breathe and swim. When he went to deep water, he had to hold onto the side. Being in the middle of the deep was not an option. Still, he said he was not afraid and that he just needed to learn to breathe.

When it came time in class to learn about breathing, Jerry followed the steps one by one. He "could do" the step that comes before adding breathing to the swimming, but he couldn't do it comfortably. Still, he was convinced that he was ready to add the breathing to the swimming.

He practiced swimming and trying to get a breath. He practiced for a few hours and became very frustrated. He didn't make a shred of progress, in his own mind.

I suggested that he go back and embody the step that came before putting breathing and swimming together. I told him I could see that he was able to perform it, but he hadn't mastered it; he was slightly ahead of himself. He politely obliged me, but he seemed to be resisting. Since he didn't feel that this was the way he should be using his time, he resumed trying to breathe while swimming. He could not slow down and embody Step 1.

He is still struggling with the breathing, years later. This is what going at his own pace requires in this case. Since I could not convince him that to succeed he must go back, he will have to learn this truth on his own—a painful lesson.

When you go "backward" to become more comfortable with the basic skills, you're doing the one essential thing—dropping further down into your body—that will prepare you for what comes next in your learning. So, going backward really is taking you a step closer to your goals. Going backward is going forward.

BY BEING IN YOUR BODY LONG ENOUGH,
YOU INEVITABLY COME TO A BREAKTHROUGH.

Many people believe that in order to swim, they simply need to learn to breathe, tread water, and move their arms correctly. But no matter how many classes they take, they don't learn. They don't know that learning to swim is about *stillness, not movement.* Few people do.

I'm repeating the point (ad nauseum?) that the goal is *comfort, not skill* because students in my classes forget it so often. It takes repetition to change a habit. Is your habit changing? Stick with me!

You won't learn the mechanics of breathing if you're afraid you won't get enough air. You won't learn to breathe if you must get to the other side, or you think the water might not hold you up, or that you might "lose it." And you won't learn to swim if you're afraid of looking silly or you feel you must learn today in order to get your money's worth or because you're going on vacation or you've just entered a triathlon. You must be in your body to learn.

SLOWING DOWN MAY BE AN UNCOMFORTABLE STEP,
BUT NOT SLOWING DOWN IS WORSE.

Fun Game: Tipping and Rolling

This is a skill that's done best with a nose clip for now. If you feel comfortable in the front float, and if it sounds like fun, see what happens when you take a breath and go into a front float and then tip sideways on purpose. Can you find a way to make yourself tip? It doesn't require thought! Just feel.

2+2=4

ALWAYS TAKE A BREATH BEFORE YOU PRACTICE
A SKILL IN THE WATER.

To tip on purpose, you can turn your head one way or the other. Or, you can place one arm across your body. See what it takes to put yourself out of balance and let yourself roll. You may end up on your side, your back, or on your front. See where imbalance takes you.

Rolling over

When you take time to play with balance, it helps you understand how your body works in the water. You'll find out, among other things, that the water holds you up no matter what creative position you get into. Important!

Seal Rolls

Seals roll over like hotdogs on a rotisserie (but faster). Lying in a front float, do something that will take you off balance. Go slowly and make being in control your goal—not rolling over. Use a nose clip.

Going slowly, now see if you can roll yourself all the way over from your front to your back, and around again to your front, like a seal. It doesn't matter if you do it—or how you do it. What matters? That you stay in your body.

IT'S MORE IMPORTANT TO REMAIN IN CONTROL
THAN IT IS TO DO A SEAL ROLL.

Use your hands—your "propellers"—to keep rolling until you have turned 360 degrees, as though you were on a rotisserie. If at any moment you feel as though you're about to do something uncomfortable, *stop*. Give yourself a moment to gather yourself. Stand up if you need to.

SWIMMING BACKWARD

From a front float, see if you can propel yourself in the direction of your feet. If your body doesn't remain in the same floating position, it's okay; your feet may drop. This toy teaches you more about propulsion.

STEP 48: BACK FLOAT PRACTICE

Spend more time in your back float. Practice getting into it, coming out of it, and the different things that come up when you do a back float. What happens when you breathe deeply? You'll want to try this with a nose clip on. Review what happens when you take a deep breath and hold it.

What happens when you let a lot of air out? What happens when you take shallow breaths but get enough air to feel comfortable?

Notice whether you're allowing your feet to go where they naturally go. Do you try to lift them off the bottom? (Since I can't see you, I have to pose this question from time to time.)

Notice whether your body feels loose as you float on your back. Is there any tension? If so, where is it? Remember to allow it to be there. Only when you allow it to be there can you return to your body. Then tension can melt away. It will, if you allow it long enough.

Step 49: Learning Time

Now and then, students get impatient with their progress. They want to know everything yesterday. They want to take a pill and be free in deep water. How are you doing with your patience? How long should it take to overcome fear of water? To learn to swim? What are your expectations?

Write your expectations here:

1. _____
2. _____
3. _____
4. _____

Although it's not *probable* that your fear will be completely healed today or tomorrow, we must hold that anything is possible. And it is.

However, the beliefs you have concerning yourself in water and in deep water had time to grow roots. When you pull weeds out of the ground (this is not to say that fear is a weed), you're careful to pull them out by the roots so they won't grow back. We do the same thing with your beliefs.

Give yourself time for the roots to loosen and pull free.

For example, you wouldn't want to force your face into the water when you really don't like having your face in, and then swim across the pool feeling tense and uncomfortable.

If you do something you don't like—such as putting your face in the water—and try to build a new skill on top of it, you divide yourself in two. You cannot be 100% present to the new skill, so you cannot learn it. Presumably you want to get to the root of the discomfort and change it to ease and comfort. *Then* you can swim across the pool, enjoying every moment.

The amount of time it will take you to overcome your fear in water is the amount of time it takes to let go of old beliefs that aren't true about the water or yourself and to learn to trust yourself in water. This is neither difficult nor mysterious.

WHEN YOU'VE BROUGHT YOUR PRESENCE FOR A SKILL OR BELIEF COMPLETELY INTO YOUR BODY, YOU'VE LEARNED IT

You'll accomplish both letting go of old beliefs and trusting yourself in the water by learning how to remain in your body. Let yourself be where you are and just *feel*. All the healing you seek in the water takes place from there.

When you're *out* of the pool, the starting point for learning is your beliefs about yourself and the water. Your beliefs determine how your body will feel when you're in the water.

When you're *in* the pool where feeling the water is obvious and present, the starting point for learning is the way you *feel*. You can feel your beliefs. Or better said, you can feel the effect of your beliefs. Your body is your feelings-gauge. Your body gives you signals, just like a traffic light does: *Stop. Go. Caution.*

When you're in the water, watch for your body's signals. When it signals caution, slow down and stop. When it signals stop, *stop!* Don't run a red light. In fact, don't run a yellow light. If you do, you're putting yourself at risk of panicking. Once you're in the 2nd or 3rd Circle, it's easier to fly out to the 5th Circle than it is if you're in the 1st Circle, focused on staying there. Keep yourself in the 1st Circle.

Don't run a red light.
Don't run a yellow light, either.

STEP 50: MAKE THE SECOND CIRCLE YOUR RED LIGHT

He ran a yellow light: he left the 1st Circle.

He regrouped.

As soon as you feel yourself outside of the 1st Circle, *stop* and regroup. Get back into the 1st Circle where you're comfortable and where you can learn.

How long will it take you to learn to swim the way you dream you can? It's different for everyone. It partially depends on how much you let things happen rather than pushing them. Are you willing to try the lessons and ideas in this book? I hope so. It will pay off, and sooner than you may have thought possible.

If you would be comfortable going to the pool to practice once a week, give yourself 8 months to a year to learn the teachings and skills in this book. It would be fruitless to hurry. This is a reasonable amount of time for this course, doing it on your own. You may learn sooner, or it could take longer. If you follow the steps, and skip none, you cannot miss. That's a promise.

STEP 51: PUSHING YOURSELF—MORE ON "GOING BACKWARD IS GOING FORWARD"

If you've been practicing something for days and nothing seems to be happening, check that you're practicing while you're in your body. If you don't seem to be making any progress, you're probably:
- pushing yourself (and therefore out of the 1st Circle)
- practicing something that's too advanced (and therefore you're tense and out of the 1st Circle)
- skipping a step, which would put you (out of the 1st Circle), or
- in the future or the past, which are also (out of the 1st Circle)

These all boil down to pushing yourself.

You cannot learn a skill when you're in the past, in the future, or you're pushing yourself. If you perform a skill once or twice, that's all well and good for the moment, but it will not "stick." You'll have to return to it and become present to it if you want to learn.

Go "backward." You're trying to go from Topeka to Denver before you've gone from Atlanta to Topeka. Go back to a step of the same skill that was completely comfortable.

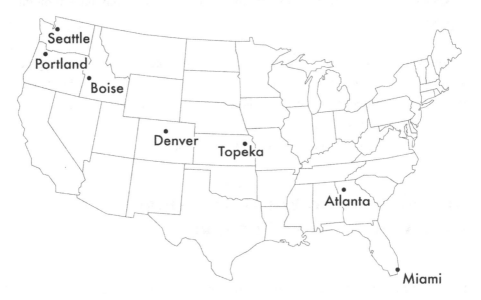

Spend more time with that step and get to know it better. Do it until you can practically do it in your sleep.

STEP 52: THE LEARNING METER

The Learning Meter measures how much learning is taking place. When you practice, where are you on the Learning Meter?

You're learning very well if you're present and comfortable. If you stay present and comfortable, learning is unstoppable.

| LOW | MEDIUM | HIGH | MASTERY |

Learning Levels on The Learning Meter

Low	Medium	High	Mastery
• Low quality of instructions	• Medium quality of instructions	• High quality of instructions	• Mastery: "Got it"
• Poor level of learning	• Moderate level of learning	• Good level of learning	• Learning level has become "owning"
• Not fun	• Hopeful	• Fun	• You feel oneness with yourself and the water. Fun.
• What am I doing here?	• I'm getting somewhere.	• I'm learning and healing.	
		• More, please.	• I have "arrived."
	to		to This figure is explained in the section on Mastery

The Learning Meter measures how much learning is taking place.
Your level of learning varies with your presence.

Quality of instruction is a measure of how well the instructions match your need. Are you met at your level? Is your question heard and is it answered correctly?

Level of learning is the progress you make due to an answer you're given. Information that's understood can be used fruitfully.

Learning doesn't always mean you're doing something new; it can also mean that you're continuing to embody something you started practicing earlier.

2+2=4

IT'S MORE ADVANCED ON THE LEARNING METER TO BE
COMFORTABLE AND NOT COMPLETE A SKILL THAN
TO COMPLETE IT AND BE UNCOMFORTABLE.

STEP 53: LEARNING PATH

We think of the learning path as being a straight line.

Step 1   Step 2   Step 3   End

But I am sure you have experienced it differently if you've been reading this book and practicing in the pool. At times, one skill leads directly into another. At other times you may find yourself taking side trips or doubling back.

A normal and perfectly good learning path can look like this:

The shape of a perfectly good and normal learning path.

For instance, you may be trying to float on your stomach at the wall. You discover that you've been kicking your feet up, trying to keep them off the bottom. This is uncomfortable, so you take a side trip to examine why. You learn that you're not supposed to kick your feet up; they go where they're supposed to go by themselves, and you don't have to help. You realize that your belief about your floating position needs to change and it does.

Or, in the middle of learning to turn over onto your back, you find that you haven't yet learned how to keep water out of your nose. So, you take a side trip to learn about nose clips or about keeping water out of your nose. When you get that down pat, turning over becomes a cinch. You advance.

WAS IT A FLUKE?

Sometimes, out of the blue you do a skill correctly that you've never done before. It's a complete surprise. It feels good, it's easy, and you know you did something right. You wonder how you got there. You want to do it again.

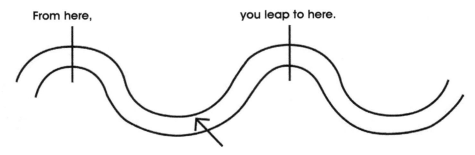

From here,   you leap to here.

Then you go back to fill in this space. This is not regressing.

You made a huge leap forward. You search your memory to see how you did it. You go into your head—and leave your body behind. But the "map" is not in your head; it's in your body. You connected to the map with your presence. You performed a new skill by doing what was fun for you in the moment. This is what you want to repeat.

To develop a map that gives you the control you need to repeat the skill on purpose, start over from the same place with the simplest plan: be present. *Let go of whether it "works" again or not.* Let the moments unfold. The breakthrough may or may not happen just as it did before. *It doesn't matter.* Be prepared to let anything happen. When something feels right, follow it. Only by coming upon it naturally—maybe five or ten times—will you realize what your body did. Let your body lead you. *The benefits of this cannot be overemphasized.*

When you discover what your body did, you are filling in the space pictured above; you're building a map. When you've let your new skill unfold by itself enough times, you'll be able to do it intentionally. *Trust your body. It knows things that your mind does not.* All you need to do is to be there and let it happen. After a while, you'll be able to do the skill on purpose.

When there are huge leaps followed by dropping back and filling in the space, this is good learning. There's no error or waste in any part of it.

When you climb a ladder, you advance by stepping on a rung and pushing your-self up. Each time you push yourself up you get closer to your goal.

When one foot is on its way to the next rung, there's no visible progress *upward*, however, it's an indispensable part of your progress.

If you can't "see" your swimming progress, look a little deeper. See if there's an increase of your presence in water, causing you to be more "there," more at ease, more one with the water, more aware. This progress is what fills the space between where you are and a leap to a new place.

Spend time embodying each step of this book. You are *always* making progress.

AT ANY MOMENT, YOU ARE EITHER ON YOUR WAY
TO THE NEXT RUNG, OR ON IT.

Step 54: Understanding "I Can"

"I can swim across the pool (but I can't wait to get to the other side)."

"I can put my face in the water (but I hate it)."

"I can exhale through my nose into the water (but I have to force myself.)" Each of these skills is being accomplished with tension.

If a swimming instructor asks you if you can do X, Y, or Z, and you have performed X, Y, or Z five times in your life, the answer to the question is not necessarily, "Yes."

If you "can" do the skills, but only uncomfortably, think of it this way: you can't do them yet. You can't do them the way we (you and I) want you to. If you're uncomfortable, you won't enjoy the skills and you probably won't relish practicing them. It would be foolhardy to try to build something new on top of them. We don't want swimming to be a chore.

"Can do" the skill means "do the skill with ease and comfort." Go back and get comfortable. Start from calm. Stay comfortable. Proceed very slowly, staying in your body. If you're proceeding slowly, then stopping the skill will also be slow and easy.

STEP 55: "PAVING NEW ROAD" EXERCISE

Make a list of the skills in which you feel *any* tension in the water. If you haven't been in the water yet, do this later.

1. _____
2. _____
3. _____
4. _____
5. _____

Use this process for each skill:
- Choose a skill and mentally review it.
- Write down the sequence of steps you see in your mind's eye.
- Imagine doing it slowly, so slowly that you see or feel every part of it.

1. _____
2. _____
3. _____
4. _____
5. _____

The first few times you imagine the skill unfolding, there may be some gaps in the "movie" in your mind: places where you don't know what comes next. The gaps may get filled in by themselves. If not, fill them in with what you would like to see.

When you have a satisfactory movie, replay it for practice. Visualizing is practicing. Feeling is practicing, too (some people feel rather than visualize).

TRUST YOUR BODY. IT KNOWS THINGS
THAT YOUR MIND DOES NOT.

STEP 56: SWIMMING ON YOUR BACK

When you feel comfortable in your back float and you know it well, you can swim on your back. For now, this means using your arms only and letting your feet trail (just let them fall). Since we can focus on only one new thing at a time, we will begin with your arms. Do this activity in part of the pool that feels completely safe so you can focus on your new movement. If you think you might go into deep water, you'll be distracted. You can have total focus on your skill only if you are completely in your body.

MAKE SURE YOU DON'T HAVE TO THINK
ABOUT STAYING OUT OF DEEP WATER.

This is the whole arm sweep for swimming on your back. Imagine that the figure is lying on his back in shallow water:

- Starting in your comfortable back float, slide your fingertips up your sides to your armpits.
- Send your hands straight outward to the sides so that your torso and arms form a "T."
- Sweep your arms through the water so that your hands come to rest at your sides. The palms of your "pancake" hands and the insides of your arms are the surfaces that push on the water. This will thrust you backward in the direction of your head.
- The sweep is horizontal, just below the surface. Your hands should not break the surface or cause a splash.
- Let yourself glide as far as your sweep takes you. You may as well get all the distance you can from each pull.

If you float horizontally in a back float, your feet will remain at the surface when you take this sweep.

If you float with your feet low or on the bottom in your back float, the thrust of your arms will cause your feet to rise up, perhaps all the way to the surface. When you lose the momentum from that arm sweep, your feet will drop back down. Let it happen. Don't worry about your legs. Be completely there for your arm sweep. There's a lot to learn from this alone. Play with it. Get to know it.

STEP 57: HOW TO KNOW WHERE YOU'RE GOING ON YOUR BACK

We don't want swimming to become a sport in which you have to wear a helmet! Open your eyes while you're on your back, if you can. When you're going somewhere on your back, remember—you have a neck! You can watch where you're going by turning your head and looking to the sides. Turning your head won't upset your float.

Using his neck, he checks his surroundings.

While you're parked in a back float, try to look all the way behind you to see a full 360 degrees. Of course, you can always stand up to see where you are.

When you're indoors, you can track your location by watching markings on the ceiling or wall. If you're outside, you may be able to sight on a pole, sun umbrella, or roof.

Avoiding Bumping into Other People

Most likely, you don't want anyone to bump into you, and you don't want to bump into anyone else. For the most part, you are in charge of this. Before you take off on your back float each time, look around. Is anyone going to reach you by the time you lie back for your float? What are the children in the pool and on the deck doing? Learning how to judge this gives you a feeling of safety. When you're on your back, you can still check when necessary. If you bump into someone, the object is to *stay in your body*. You don't *have to* get flustered. Feel what's happening and let yourself handle it. The right thing will come to you, whether it's to stand up or to swim around someone.

Changing Direction on Your Back

What do you think will happen if you sweep just one arm as you swim on your back? Try it a few times. Try it with the other arm. It will work best if your sweeps are horizontal, as mentioned before. If you sweep downward, you'll find yourself bouncing upward out of the water and then coming back down.

If you're changing direction involuntarily, perhaps your sweeps are not symmetrical. Or, your head could be tilted to one side.

Practice changing direction on your back so you feel in control of where you go. Give yourself plenty of time to play with this. Let your legs just follow you around.

MORE GAMES ON YOUR BACK

There's plenty you can do to familiarize yourself with how the water works while you're on your back.

1. From a back float, see if you can propel yourself in the direction of your feet. This may feel awkward. Its awkwardness is one reason that it's not used as a stroke. Still, it's informative—and it might make you chuckle.

2. From a back float, see if you can roll over onto your front. It's like rolling over in bed.

Rolling from back float to front float

ROLLING OVER TO REST ON YOUR BACK

If you knew how to be in control, and you could roll over from your front float to your back float, and you knew how to rest in a back float, you could *get air whenever you wanted it in deep water*. This next skill is a good one

191

to practice using a nose clip until you've got it down. If you did the seal rolls above, you probably already have it.

To review, if you aren't in your body for a front or back float yet, go back to that section to learn it.

From your happy front float, ask your body to turn over. Your body will respond well. Because you're in your body, you have control over this. You'll intuitively know how to start rolling. It doesn't matter if you finish.

WE DON'T CARE IF YOU ROLL OVER.
WE ONLY CARE THAT YOU REMAIN IN CONTROL.

As you begin to roll, check in with yourself. Is it okay to be on your side? If so, go ahead. When you get to your back, tip your head back enough that your face will be out of the water. Lie in your back float with your head in a comfortable position. There is such a thing as putting your head back too far: your eyes go under water. Just make your face and neck comfortable.

If you didn't make it all the way around, but you stayed in the 1st Circle, *great*.

If you made it all the way around, but you felt panicky, you forgot to put comfort first. Do that next time.

IT'S MORE ADVANCED TO REMAIN IN CONTROL
AND ABORT A SKILL THAN TO COMPLETE
THE SKILL AND LOSE CONTROL

Why? Because the goal is to remain in the 1st Circle *all the time*. This is what makes you safe. It's *this* that creates a safe swimmer.

Yes, there's an in-between stage, the stage of uncertainty that can fall between control and fear. Uncertainty, as long as you feel safe, is okay.

TRAP

If you said to yourself, "I want to learn this without my nose clip," and you took it off and proceeded to get water in your nose, you demonstrated the method to my madness: focusing on rolling over, you no longer could protect your nose. You can only be in one place: in the roll, or in your nose.

If you anticipate getting water in your nose *next time*, you'll be focused on protecting your nose and won't be able to focus on rolling over then, either. I suggest you wear a nose clip until blipping becomes a habit. Practice that alone.

STEP 58: COORDINATION

What does "coordinated" mean? It means moving in an organized way. It means you and your body are synchronized. It means being in your body— you and your body moving as one. How can you become coordinated? By listening to your body.

If you're pushing yourself, you probably won't move in a coordinated way. Sometimes you're "moving" so fast you don't notice that you're out of your body. Slow down and feel what your body is doing.

Let's say you're learning the back float. You feel the water supporting you and you know you're floating. Your inquisitive self asks, "Can I swim on my back to there?" If you're in your body, swimming there is a cinch. You feel in control. Your balance is there. You can feel the progress of each stroke. It's not tiring, and it feels coordinated. If you're not in your body, you may get there, but it won't feel good. You might notice that your stomach is tight, your neck is stiff, or your balance is off. Don't swim on your back until you can do it comfortably. Come home first. Comfort allows coordination.

If adding your arms to a back float—even though you don't have your back float down yet—sounds like too much fun to pass up, then go ahead and try it. But be prepared: it's possible that you'll leave the 1st Circle.

Remember, when one skill becomes part of you—when you embody it— you can fix your attention on something else. When you embody the second skill, the two will be coordinated. Surely you don't think you could fail at learning anything. This is a formula for success: you can learn any skill if you're present.

WHEN YOU'RE IN YOUR BODY, IT BECOMES
POSSIBLE FOR THINGS TO BECOME COORDINATED.

STEP 59: BREATH

It's not time to learn to breathe as you swim yet, but let's get started with the elementary points.

EVERYDAY BREATHING

As you sit in your chair, there are two main parts of your breathing: inhaling and exhaling. Both take about the same amount of time. However, it takes much more time and effort to exhale into the water than it takes to exhale into air. This is because water is much denser than air. You have to push your air into the water.

On land we breathe through the nose most of the time. However, while swimming, we breathe in through the mouth, because the opening is big, allowing inhalation to be swift. Usually, we breathe *out* through the nose because this prevents water from coming into the nose.

BREATH EXERCISES

Stand in a place in the pool where you feel completely safe and grounded. Feel free to hold onto the wall for stability.

If you're not comfortable putting your face in water, go back to that section of the book and build the skill slowly. You can't fail if you go at your own pace and skip no steps. There's plenty of time.

As you stand in the pool, imagine yourself inhaling a comfortable breath through your mouth and exhaling into the water through your nose. If you want to use a nose clip, that's fine; you'll exhale through your mouth. Imagine that you have plenty of air and you've lowered your face into the water. Visualize blowing your air out, causing bubbles to pop up all around your face. The harder you blow, the louder and bigger the bubbles will be. The softer you blow, the quieter and smaller.

When you can see this in your mind's eye and you're ready to experiment, try these games.

BREATH AND NOSE TOYS

1. Standing with your face above the water, begin to exhale. Lower your face down to the water and, still exhaling, (preferably through the nose, but if necessary, through the mouth), dip your face in and bring it right back out. Keep exhaling the whole time. See if it's okay to exhale into the water for this brief amount of time. Do this a number of times until it becomes old hat. If your air doesn't want to come out, see "Troubleshooting Breathing" a few pages ahead.

2. Exhale short bursts of air outward into the water. Feel what part of your body stops the exhalations.

3. Exhale into the water through your mouth with your lips pursed. Notice how long your exhalation takes. Then exhale into the water with your mouth wide open. Notice how long your exhalation takes.

4. Exhale into the water through your mouth or nose. Stop exhaling in the middle of your breath. Then resume exhaling.

5. When you come up for air, see what happens if you inhale through your nose instead of through your mouth. Anything?

6. Exhale through your nose into the water. *Let* air come out instead of pushing it out. Come up and inhale through your mouth. Repeat this as long as you're having fun.

7. Exhale through your nose into the air and feel the warmth in your nose as compared to the coolness of inhaling through your nose.

8. Take the biggest breath you can. Exhale through your nose into the water as slowly as you can.

9. Do #8 once again, but this time exhale at a normal rate. Notice how long it takes to exhale to the end of a normal, comfortable exhalation.

10. Take a deep breath and hold it. Time how long you can hold it.

11. Take a deep breath. Then exhale all your air into the air, every last wisp of air you can push out. At the very end, without inhaling, time how long you can remain at the end of your breath before you must inhale. After you've done it, notice that you're still alive.

Give yourself many practices with each breathing toy. The idea of these toys is to get to know your breath capacity and gain control over your breath. Once you have control over your breath, it gives you more freedom to play in the water.

STEP 60: WATER RUNNING OFF YOUR FACE

When you come up, water will run off your face. A small amount may run into your mouth as you open your mouth for a breath. Take time to feel this. It will not interfere with your inhalation. If you have a lot of hair, more water will drain off your face and into your mouth unless you tie back your hair or wear a swim cap. The water usually ends up under your tongue, the lowest part of your mouth. Go ahead and take your next breath, then go under and expel the water from your mouth. Do this by squirting it out (not spitting). You don't even have to open your mouth. Barely parting your lips is enough. Then finish exhaling your air until your body tells you to come up.

STEP 61: BREATHING

Take a comfortable breath and exhale into the water again. When it's time to come up, do so and take a new breath. Return to exhaling into the water. Continue this for a while. You'll inhale and exhale the same amount: what comes in must go out. If your air exchange is even, you'll be able to continue this indefinitely. If it's not even, you'll get winded.

As you exhale, feel the air in your lungs decreasing. Since you're in your body, your body will keep you from coming up too soon or too late.

Find a slow, comfortable, easy pace. It might change now and then. It should feel easy and natural. Do we care if you inhale air and exhale into the water? No, we don't. We only care that you feel comfortable and in control— that you're in the 1st Circle. Agreed? See how long you can go up and down breathing this way without getting tired.

You cannot force all the air in your body out of your lungs. There will always be a residual amount of air left in your lungs that prevents them from collapsing. If you feel out of breath in the water, remember that you still have this residual air to live on. You might want to get air right away, and that's okay, but it would not be time to panic yet! (You know I'm kidding, right? It's never time to panic…unless you let yourself go).

TROUBLESHOOTING BREATHING

1. If you don't like exhaling through your nose, exhale through your mouth. It will work just as well in the position you're using for this exercise (head vertical or slightly forward). You can exhale through your nose later. Do what's comfortable now!

2. Let's say you want to exhale into the water and your breath stops short: it doesn't want to come out. That's okay. Give it your full permission to stop. Let it be stuck. Give yourself plenty of time to feel what's happening when it stops coming out.

When you've done this for a few minutes—and you feel as though you understand it—see if you can stop exhaling on purpose. Do this for a few more minutes. It's not worthwhile to force yourself to blow out the air. Forcing yourself would be putting yourself outside the 1st Circle. That doesn't work in the long run. Practice being in the 1st Circle all the time. Being in control is more important than "getting it done."

3. If You Get Tired, Out of Breath, or Lightheaded

If your air exchange is not even, that is, if what comes in is more than what goes out, you'll become winded, out of breath. This is the most common problem for people who have learned to "swim" but who "cannot get the breathing." They don't realize how much air they must breathe out to make it work. Take more time to exhale while your face is in the water. Or, exhale faster.

If you exhale more than you inhale, you'll get lightheaded over time. Slow down and regroup. Make your air exchange comfortable.

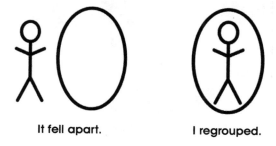

It fell apart.   **I regrouped.**

If you still don't like putting your face in water, forget about learning the breathing for now. Go back and take the appropriate steps *from where you are now.*

The goal of this breathing exercise is to be able to exhale into the water and come up for air repeatedly, for minutes at a time, without getting tired. It becomes a meditative, comfortable exercise. Eventually, you'll be able to breathe out through your nose and mouth interchangeably. You might prefer to exhale through your nose since this prevents water from entering your nose.

Often, people try to keep a rhythm in breathing exercises. This can be a mistake because they put the rhythm ahead of feeling comfortable. If you let yourself stay comfortable, there will be a loose rhythm. Comfort is the goal, not rhythm.

STEP 62: CHAIR TOY

Try this new position. After taking a breath, sit in the water as though you were on a lawn chair but with your feet slightly out in front of you on the bottom.

Go into a sitting position as though you're in a chair.
Your arms may float like this, or lower. Both are okay.

Lean back just slightly. Keep your head vertical, so you won't risk getting water in your nose. Your face will be partially or fully submerged. If you find that your feet float up or your face does not submerge, raise your arms vertically overhead.

Raising your arms overhead pushes you down since they can't float in the air.

The weight of your arms above the surface will push your body slightly downward. This should cause your feet to reach the bottom if they hadn't already. If they're still floating, that's okay. Find your balance.

Take time to get your balance. Practice this chair position for a few minutes, standing up for air when you need to. Go slowly. Become comfortable with holding your breath and coming up to rest whenever you need to. Do this until you've got it down.

Now try this. (This is a good time to use a nose clip.) Putting your arms in the water just below the surface and using your "pancake hands" (your flat palms and the whole inside surface of your arms), sweep downward on the water toward the bottom and see what happens.

Ready to sweep downward with the largest surface area possible.

After the downward sweep.

What happened? Did you get the result you expected? If all went according to plan, you pushed yourself up and out of the water. Your chin came above the surface.

The faster you push downward, the higher up you'll go. If you push down very, very slowly, you may find no rise whatsoever. Experiment with different speeds and pressures and see their effects.

The point is to lift yourself above the surface, then to let gravity draw you back down.

NOTE: Your hands should be held in line with your forearms: pancake hands and no bending at the wrist, or you'll lose your purchase on the water. What is "purchase?" It's the hold you have on the water, or the "grip" you get on it, or the "traction" you get when you push on it.

Good hand position: keep your hand this way. Flat as a pancake
(both the back of the hand and the palm are flat). Recall that
the thumb doesn't need to be next to the forefinger.

If your hands are in any of the following positions, they will be much less effective:

Hand bent downward: you have less purchase on the water.

Hands cupped: you lose more purchase on the water.

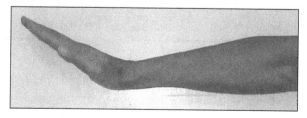

Hand bent upward: you lose even more purchase on the water.

When you rise above the surface as a result of your arm sweep, you stay up for a moment. Then gravity takes over and you drop back below the surface. When you go back under water, you could get water in your nose if you didn't wear a nose clip, so the clip is recommended. If you simply cannot find one, then go back and learn to blip. A nose clip is a step, not a crutch!

Gravity takes you back under water as low as your buoyancy will allow. Then, buoyancy takes over and you start floating upward again. Gravity. Buoyancy. Gravity. Buoyancy. These are the two natural forces we play with in the water. Did you notice this? You have to *wait* for your body to go down and come back up. When you've begun to float back up, *ask your body* when you should make your arm sweep downward. *Your body will tell you.* Practice this. It's important. When you spend time with these two natural forces, going up and down, you'll see how little effort is needed to bring yourself above the water.

If you find yourself coming up too slowly, you probably need to take a bigger breath first. If you're a sinker, you won't float back up: it may take you two or three arm strokes to come back above the surface. Whatever works is okay.

As we said earlier, two things make you float: air and fat. Remember, whenever you begin to practice something in the water, take a breath just before you go under: it gives you added buoyancy. You'll find yourself taking the breath through your mouth simply because it's quick and convenient, not because you're in a hurry.

During this exercise, you're holding your breath the whole time (and wearing a nose clip) so you can focus on one thing: going up and down. Go down with gravity. Come up by using buoyancy first, *then* your arm sweep. Repeat this until it feels easy and natural. Stand up to rest when needed. Give yourself days to learn this.

When you rise toward the surface each time, you can feel that the water does most of the work. You can rely on this. Part of its reliability depends on the fact that you have air in your lungs. The more air you have, the sooner and faster you'll come up. You add just a little effort with your arm sweep at the end of your buoyant ascent.

Experiment with different amounts of air. You don't need to come out of the water to your navel. Just come out so that your chin clears the surface.

I call this exercise "bouncing off the water." It's as though you're bouncing off an imaginary line in the water where gravity loses its pull and your buoyancy takes over (the point where you stop going down and start coming back up).

She's on her way down, then, BOING!
She bounces off an imaginary line.
Let the water do the work.

When you become comfortable with this skill, you will have learned the first steps of getting yourself into position to get air. *Do not push yourself. Don't get ahead of yourself.*

STEP 63: FALLING TOYS, WHALE JUMPS, QUARTERS

Stand with your arms at your sides in chest-deep water. If it sounds like fun, fall forward into the water keeping your body in line (straight) and see what the water does with you. It will be a very slow, gentle fall to the surface as though you're falling into Jell-O.

He was in waist-deep water for this fall.
He had already done it in chest-deep water.

Do this five or ten times. Get the feeling of falling, what to expect, and what happens after you "land." Then move to water that's five or six inches shallower. Fall into the water again with your hands at your sides. Get the feeling of falling from this "height." Learn what to expect and what happens after you "land."

Go to water that's waist deep. Fall into the water with your hands at your sides. You won't hit the bottom or even come close. Your head will most likely not even go under water. Get the feeling of falling from this "height." Learn what to expect and what happens after you "land."

Are you getting an idea of how resilient the water is? How dense a mattress it is, relative to air? How you can depend on it to catch you and hold you up? Can you allow the water to have you, without any resistance on your part?

You can even go to water that's knee-deep and do the same exercise. If you keep your body straight, you'll still land on the water and your head will barely go beneath the surface, if at all. Sound like fun? If not, you can work down to this depth, a few inches at a time to prove to yourself that you're safe.

FALLING SIDEWAYS TOY

In chest-deep water, practice falling sideways into the water. You may want to use a nose clip or hold your nose. See how it feels to fall sideways. See what your body does. Where do you end up? Then do it in waist-deep water.

DO WE CARE IF YOU FALL IN SIDEWAYS? NO.

We only care that you feel completely in control. If falling in sideways sounds like something that would cause you to lose control, then naturally you wouldn't do it. To make it easier to fall in sideways, you may prefer to start with your shoulders under water so you're falling from a lower point. It's more important to stay in the 1st Circle than to fall. Don't do anything that would cause you to leave the 1st Circle unless it sounds like fun.

REVIEW

Question: "But if it's not comfortable, shouldn't I practice it until it becomes comfortable?"

Answer: *No. Does it make sense that practicing discomfort would make you comfortable?* Remember, you're all too familiar with being uncomfortable and out of control. It has not made you happy: it's kept you from learning. Practice comfort. The messages of this book are so reliable that in our classes, we guarantee that people will learn to swim as long as they try the teaching.

To try it is to be convinced. Learning to swim is learning to be in the 1st Circle in the water all the time. So, practice it.

Whale Jumps

Have you ever seen a whale breaching? It looks like this:

Two whales breaching

Using a nose clip, start with your own mini-whale jumps. If you've mastered the Falling Sideways toy, then crouch a bit, take a little jump, and let yourself fall sideways. Do this for a while, becoming more and more confident (in-your-body) as you do.

Then, be like a child and do a whale jump. Crouch down in the water and launch yourself with reckless abandon out of the water sideways, backward, or forward. Let gravity take you where it will, and let buoyancy bring you back to the surface. There's no work for you to do once you've launched. A nose clip prevents you from having to be concerned about getting water in your nose. Or, hold your nose.

Whale jump

How can you look dignified and self-respecting doing whale jumps in a public pool? Well, you can't. But if it's okay with you, it will be okay with others. It's just fun and, it pays off. Here's Nina coming back down from a whale jump.

Mid whale jump

QUARTERS TOY

Throw a quarter to the bottom of the pool.

Go get it. You'll find a way to get it, one way or another.

To make it more challenging, throw it into chest deep water.

To make it more challenging, throw more than one coin in. Count what you throw in. To make it more challenging, throw in smaller coins that are harder to pick up.

What did you learn?

STEP 64: HOW DOES FEAR HEAL?

To become free in water, there are two things to do: stay in the 1st Circle and learn how the water works.

If you stay in the 1st Circle, fear cannot overtake you. As you show yourself you can do things in the 1st Circle, fear gives way to confidence. Skip no steps. Let's illuminate the steps of healing fear.

There are three things to do with any fear: avoid it, manage it, and heal it. It seems that most people either avoid it or manage it. Healing it seems to be such a mystery that few people try. Individuals and therapeutic relationships try to heal fear. Some succeed. Institutions such as government, the media, business, and medicine don't usually try; they only hope to manage it. Swimming lessons as a whole manage it, too: "Don't be afraid." "Learn strokes and treading." These seldom work.

As far as I have seen in over 40 years as an instructor, managing fear does not satisfy adult learn-to-swim students. It doesn't allow a person to be comfortable: in his body and happy. It eventually leads students to find reasons to skip swimming.

The benefit of avoiding fear is self-evident: it feels better. But it only feels better in the short term. But it doesn't help make you safe around water. Over time, avoiding fear is tiresome and disappointing. It can erode self esteem. When we avoid fear, we miss the opportunity to have a successful, empowering experience—and to permanently change our lives for the better.

If everyone knew that it's safe to confront fear, that there is a step-by-step process that would not be forced upon them and which they could take at their own pace, a process that's simple, easy and fun that *always* works, then maybe we would all be more enthused about facing our fears. Obviously, moving from fear to confidence is extremely life-enhancing. Is there such a way for us all to *heal fear?* Yes.

HEALING FEAR IS THE WAY OUT.

Healing fear is a learning process. *It's simple.* It can take a short while or a long while. If correct steps are followed and none are skipped, it's inevitable and predictable. You can't possibly fail any more than 2+2 can fail to equal 4.

WHAT DOES IT MEAN TO LOSE CONTROL?

A way to define fear is "uncertainty that you will be able to remain in control or be safe." There is one important thing to bear in mind throughout your learning process: *fear is not your fault.*

When we're in the 1st Circle, we're in our bodies. We control what we do. When we leave our bodies—even a little bit—we begin to lose control. In the 2nd Circle, we have most of our control but not all of it. In the 3rd Circle, we're "losing it." In the 4th Circle we have lost almost all physical control; and in the 5th Circle, we've "lost it:" lost all control.

Once you know you can stay in your body to prevent the loss of control, you have a power that children and panicking people don't have. Usually when we're afraid, we're at least able to do what's needed to survive. But more power is available to us.

You and I don't ever *lose* control. We give it up. We let ourselves go to the 5th Circle. It's not a bad thing but it causes an injury we don't notice until later. We let ourselves leave in order to avoid pain. Because it feels better, to avoid pain, it becomes a habit. *This is good news.* It means that we *can* be in charge of our experience once we learn how to remain in control. It may feel as though we lose control, but that's only because we didn't know we had the power to keep it.

LOSING CONTROL IS ACTUALLY GIVING UP CONTROL

- Keeping it means staying in our bodies.
- Out-of-control is out of your body.
- Control is a location.
- Staying in control—in our bodies—requires going slowly and continuing to feel.

Sometimes we are so in the habit of giving away control that it takes a lot of focus to "stay here" in the 1st Circle. Sometimes it's so scary to stay here that we can do it only if we know that someone else will keep us safe. At my swim school, this person is called a spotter.

On the left: a spotter, present and trustworthy. The student goes at his own pace. In this exercise, he's learning to feel the water hold him up. He determines the hand grip or lack of one.

From my experience, there's no person of normal physical and mental means who cannot overcome any fear of anything or learn anything if the proper environment of safety and the proper steps are provided. And you're the one who determines what is safe for you. Therefore, no matter how much fear of deep (or shallow) water you have, you can overcome it and be free... and learn to swim with total comfort, confidence, and ease.

In control: watching an under water demonstration

Healing Fear

Let's dive into the statement, "Fear is not your fault."

If an adult is afraid in water, something happened to cause it. It doesn't come from nowhere. It is not silly.

And though I wasn't there, I can be sure of several things:
- the person doesn't trust him/herself in water;
- he doesn't know how the water works—or if he once knew, he's forgotten;
- he doesn't want to feel out of control again, and;
- either he hopes to heal his fear or he has given up on being safe in water.

Many people have given up because when they tried to fix their fear, they were taught strokes instead. Strokes are irrelevant. Such efforts are so discouraging that often people don't go back. To be taught correctly and thoroughly, an instructor must be well-trained in the steps of overcoming fear and learning.

Let's use an all-too-common example of how fear in water begins.

Tim has been afraid in water ever since he was a little boy when his older brother held him under water too long while they were horsing around in the pool. Timmy was stuck under water and could not come up when he wanted to. He experienced the extreme discomfort of helplessness, frustration, anger, desperation, fear, and panic—the 5th Circle.

When his brother, John, finally let him up, Timmy punched his brother, cried, yelled at him, and told their parents. Punching his brother and yelling were helpful to release some of the tremendous energy that built inside him during this transgression. Telling their parents was helpful if they responded appropriately. Timmy needed to know his parents were on his side and John needed to know he was wrong. These help Timmy regain his equilibrium. He can talk about his feelings until all the conversation, emoting, and hopefully an apology from John restore him as much as they can.

But there's something else that is not regained. It doesn't take place between Timmy and another. It takes place in him. But neither he nor his family nor his future swimming instructors know about it.

When Timmy felt so desperately out of control under water beyond the capacity of his breath, he did what anyone in that situation would do: he left his body (went to the 5th Circle). It simply felt too bad to stay.

It's not that he said, "This is so bad, I'm leaving." Below the level of conscious thought, he had a "choice" of staying present or relinquishing control—a defense mechanism humans have to escape pain. He left, but not as a conscious choice. It was surrender. It was much easier than staying. It worked. We all do it. It's okay.

To stay in our bodies with that much discomfort is virtually impossible for us. That is, until we learn how and learn that it's worthwhile. We "have" to leave, and we do. However, to leave our bodies is to abandon them and our safety. We can't be in control of what our bodies do if we're not in them. But then we also must not blame ourselves for it.

> WE HAVE TO LEAVE, AND WE DO.
> BUT THEN WE MUST NOT BLAME OURSELVES FOR IT.

When we did it, it was the best option in the moment. When we must abandon our body, or believe we must, we owe it to ourselves to then let ourselves off the hook for it. It's only fair. We are innocent.

After time has gone by and reevaluation has taken place, we need to learn how to handle it another way if it happens again. That means learning to stay in the 1st Circle.

If we don't attend to this, we become afraid that we'll leave our bodies if it happens again. This happened to Tim. That's why he's afraid in water today.

Did this happen to you? Did you let yourself off the hook? Are you willing to?

In the case of Timmy, the parents ideally would have preempted the transgression by teaching both kids that even in play, they may never hold someone under water.

My classes have led me to conclude that virtually anyone who went to the 5th Circle in the water is afraid in water today. That is, unless they knew how to heal it. Some people try getting back on the horse in hopes that it will cancel the damage. But getting back on the horse is managing fear, not healing it.

Blaming Yourself

If we hold something against ourselves, it separates us from our body. With blame, we hatch a new fear: "I might do that again. I'm not in control of not doing it again."

Blame
Body, Wedge (incident), Self.
Holding something against ourselves
keeps us out of our bodies.

The wedge prevents us from being in our body.

Holding something against ourselves is a main cause of fear. The words tell us what we're doing: holding ourselves out of our own body with a memory and our interpretation of it. But leaving our bodies when we're terrified is innocent! It deserves its own word. I call it an *inno*.

The wedge has to go. If you've already let yourself off the hook, you're done. You've changed at the Being level. You can be certain that effortless changes will follow on the Doing and Having levels.

If you need more assistance with this, see the exercises in the Appendix, page 301.

STEP 65: PREVENT PANIC, PREVENT DROWNING

We have discussed what panic is: the movement of a person from the 1st Circle to the 5th Circle. Panic is not necessary once we know what it is and how to remain comfortable—the opposite of panic. This takes practice.

Before we know the 5 Circles and how to avoid the 3rd, 4th, and 5th, we panic out of habit. Please don't feel badly about this. We all do it in parts of our lives! Panic is unavoidable while we're in the throes of the habit. Preventing it—breaking the habit—is the teaching of this book.

It's not that a book is all anyone needs to learn to swim. Using this book to teach oneself to swim has worked for many. Others need assistance mastering new ideas and habits. What ideas and habits in water do you want to master?

1. _____

2. _____

3. _____

4. _____

5. _____

6. _____

7. _____

To prevent drowning, learn the simple skills of staying in the 1st Circle and the back float in deep water. Then word will spread that learning to swim is simple and fun and it works for everyone. The world's drowning rate will plummet.

PREVENTING DROWNING IS EASIER THAN YOU THOUGHT

There are two kinds of drownings: preventable and unpreventable.

Drowning is usually due to a mistake. The vast majority of drownings are preventable. Of the 876 drownings that happen in the world every single day on average, I will guess that 858 of them–98%—are due to lack of information. Presumably, you would get the needed information from traditional swimming lessons. However, many people don't take lessons and most traditional swim instructors are trained to teach strokes rather than the essentials: how the water works, and the 5 Circles. I look forward to the day when these comprise the curriculum of all Beginning Swimming courses.

Unpreventable drownings are few and far between—those in which no matter what someone knows and does, s/he cannot prevent death. They are accidents in which something prevents someone from getting air:

1. a medical event, like a heart attack
2. trapped under water
3. air supply ends while under water

Here are examples of preventable drownings:
- falling out of a boat, into a pool, off a dock
- jumping out of a boat to save the dog
- children wandering into a back yard pool or falling into a full bucket
- ferries and tourist boats sinking, boats capsizing
- trying to save someone without taking a flotation device
- leaving a child alone in the tub "just for a second"
- rip currents
- panic

Preventable drownings are vastly more common. They're a mistake due to the lack of two bits of information: understanding how the water works and knowing how to stay in the 1st Circle (prevent panic). Panic is likely the main cause of drowning in adults. Here are some scenarios in which drowning could be avoided if the swimmer were informed:

1. You drop below the surface with the natural bobbing motion of being in water, and you mistakenly think you're stuck there; you believe you'll sink to the bottom or you don't know how to bring yourself up.

2. You don't know that water pushes you up. (It wouldn't push you up if you're one of the few true sinkers, but you can bring yourself up).

3. You don't know how to float on your back to rest.

4. Panic: a huge mobilization of energy as the body goes on high alert and you struggle or, if you're in the 4th Circle, no movement is possible because you are paralyzed by fear.

5. You don't know that by pushing down with your arms/hands or legs, you'll rise above the surface even if you are a true sinker.

6. You don't know that as you rise from being below the surface, if you EXHALE your old breath just before you break through the surface, you'll make room in your lungs for a new breath once you're up.

7. You don't know how to keep your head above water for 2-3 seconds once you're at the surface to exhale your old breath and inhale a new one IN CASE YOU DON'T exhale your old breath on the way up.

8. You don't know that if you're vertical, it's normal that only your eyes may be above the surface for a second or two before gravity causes your face to go under again by a few inches and that this is not an emergency.

9. You keep yourself under water by struggling because you don't know how easy it is to get air: how close air is, how to make room in your lungs to receive it, and how to rise a few inches to get it. And that you can lie on your back and float from a vertical float.

10. Pushing yourself too far in a game or test rather than knowing your limitations.

11. Drinking / substance intoxication and losing good judgment or balance.

12. You don't know how to keep water out of your nose and you take on too much to stay in control.

To prevent yourself from drowning in the case of a surprise water episode, you need to know how the water works and how to prevent panic. Take your time with this book and the water: you will learn the information to become safe. Do you agree that you need it?

FREQUENTLY ASKED QUESTIONS

What is drowning?

"Drowning is the process of experiencing respiratory impairment from submersion or immersion in liquid. Not all drownings are fatal."

"Fatal drowning happens when the drowning results in death. Nonfatal drowning happens when a person survives a drowning incident with a range of outcomes, from no injuries to very serious injuries or permanent disability." —Website of the Centers for Disease Control and Prevention

This definition replaces the former one most commonly understood as submersion in water resulting in death.

When would it be advisable to wear a life vest as a beginner swimmer?

In a boat: always. Additionally: anytime there is any chance that a beginner swimmer might find him/herself out of control in water— unless s/he is under supervision. The point is for the beginner to feel and be in control all the time.

Are you more at risk for drowning at night?

Not due to the water. However, the risk is higher if you have to be found in the water at night, or your faculties are impaired or you are more afraid at night.

What is a riptide?

Actually, at the beach it's called a rip current. It's a narrow current flowing away from the beach through the breakers. Though there are often breakers and wind blowing toward the beach, a rip current is formed only occasionally depending on the wind and the contour of the sea bottom.

What do you do if you get caught in a rip?

Do NOT swim against it. It won't pull you under.

1. Swim parallel to shore. You'll be drifting further from shore as you do this, but you'll get out of the current into calm water. From there, signal for help (wave, call) or slowly swim back to shore.

2. Or, don't swim. Just lie on your back as though your head were on your pillow and ride it peacefully. Eighty percent of the time, the current curves around and brings you back to shore! The other twenty percent of the time, signal for help (wave, call) or slowly swim back to shore. You are not a weanie if you call for help!

How do you get caught in a rip current:
- By not paying attention to posted signs
- By not knowing what a rip current looks and feels like
- By taking chances, thinking, "It won't happen to me."

Should you leave the water if it's raining or there's a storm?

If it's raining: no. If the rain will precede thunder and lightning, yes. If you're not sure, leave. Leave the water and be off the beach before thunder and lightning arrive.

USAGE OF SWIMMING WORDS

As you familiarize yourself with the culture of swimming, let's review some swimming words that are often misspelled or misused.

SWIM SWAM SWUM

I swim every day. Yesterday I swam.

I haven't swum in 30 years.

Not: I haven't swam in 30 years. Or, I swum yesterday.

SINK SANK SUNK SUNKEN

When I hold onto this brick, I sink.

The boat sank off the coast of Florida.

A boat was sunk off the coast of Florida to create a new SCUBA diving site.

We couldn't see the dock after the storm; it had sunk.

There are many sunken ships off the coast of North Carolina to see while SCUBA diving.

DROWN DROWNING DROWNED

She doesn't want to take a chance that she'll drown, so she's overcoming her fear of deep water.

When he was a child, he witnessed a drowning.

Last year, an average of 11 people drowned daily in the United States.

Not: My cousin drowneded when I was five.

BREATH BREATHE

I take a breath before I go under water.

I can't breathe when I swim, so I hold my breath for the whole lap.

Step 66: Pool Etiquette

As a swimming student, you may feel as though you are the "low person on the totem pole" at the pool. You aren't! You are a noble and worthy guest. Stand tall and proud and do what you went to do. Others owe you your share of space, as you owe them theirs. Sharing is the custom.

When you choose a time to practice at a pool, you may be able to choose among lap swim periods, free swim periods, adult swimming lessons, or water-walking sessions. If you go to a lap-swim period, you'll want to choose a "slow" lane. The right-of-way is indeed given to someone swimming laps.

If there's one person in your lane with you, you can share the lane, meaning that each of you takes half the lane: you stay on the left and she swims on the right, for example. If there are already two or more swimmers in the lane, avoid that lane for learning. Of course, if you are sharing the lane with one person and the third person arrives, you have a right to stay.

If you're at a water-walking session, ask the person/people in the lane if you can share the space. Your practice space will probably be small at first, but when you begin to swim, you'll need more room. Your lane-mates may grant it if you, too, are gracious.

If you choose a free-swim period when lots of kids are jumping into the pool and there's a lot of noise and activity, you might want to lay claim to a corner. This will show people that this is your space for a while. They may notice and they may not. Your best bet may be to go to a pool during off hours. Gym and hotel pools are typically underutilized much of the time as well.

Step 67: Care and Feeding of Your Swimming Instructor

After you have mastered the information in this book—in other words, you can do everything in it with confidence and ease—you'll be ready to take a traditional beginning swimming class. Perhaps some instructors will consider you more advanced and put you into an intermediate class. Whatever course you end up in, there may be things you know that the instructor is not familiar with. It may take a few years until the terminology of being in your body and the priority of comfort are common knowledge among instructors. It will be your job to tell the instructor what you need.

It's not that Miracle Swimming is the only system that produces swimmers who were once afraid and who now can swim freely in the deep. We just don't know of any other school that *teaches* you how the water works and how to prevent panic, be safe, and remain in control.

Here are some guidelines:

1. You might tell your instructor that:

    X months/years ago, you were an adult who was afraid in water. You learned that the skill that was missing was the ability to be in control in water. Now, you have learned how to *be* in control and how to *remain* in control. You're comfortable with the following skills (list them). You now wish to learn how to do Y. The way you want to learn to do Y is by making your first priority being comfortable (staying in control).

Ask: Is the instructor willing to support this?

This way, you'll keep yourself safe in this new environment. It will also bring a new awareness to the instructor, one that we hope all instructors will embrace.

2. As you listen to instructions from an instructor, listen for the things you can do and still remain safe. You may need to translate what she/he is saying into 2+2=4 language or an equivalent that feels comfortable to you.

When she says, "Kick your feet like this," translate that to, "If I can remain in control and be comfortable, kick my feet like this. But control and comfort are more important than what my feet do. If I feel afraid, I will stop." Always make comfort your first priority, no matter what the instructions are. It's okay to say, "If you don't mind, I'd like to practice comfort first." Hopefully one day, any instructor you choose will tell *you* to be comfortable first.

There is one more essential component of learning besides being in control and having fun: that is, taking responsibility for your learning. As in any class, learning depends on the relevance of the material presented, attending all of it, listening, understanding, asking all your questions, practicing the 1st Circle, asking for help when you need it, and giving yourself the time you need. If you do these things, you are assured of getting what you came for and being pleased.

STEP 68: DISPELLING BELIEFS YOU NO LONGER WANT

We've covered your beliefs and the necessity of having beliefs that support the experiences you want. This means that some of the beliefs you read earlier in this book need to change.

Some of them may have changed since then. If you'd like to help other beliefs change, here's one way. Test your belief in a safe environment slowly and carefully. Give yourself the experience that your belief is false. You may need a spotter. Only test the part that you can remain in the 1st Circle for!

_____ If I put my face in water, I'll get water in my nose or mouth.

By now, you may have put your face in the water numerous times. You may have learned to keep water out of your nose and mouth or use a nose clip. If you feel that you've achieved control with this skill, the belief has probably already changed. If not, see what happens if, when you remain in control, you put your face in water.

_____ It's dangerous when I get water in my nose or mouth.

This, too, has probably come up more than once. Do you know how to remain in control for this now?

_____ If water gets into my mouth, I'll swallow it.

_____ If I get water in my nose or mouth, I'll struggle, sputter, cough, and possibly drown.

You can try letting water into your mouth and seeing if you can remain in control. You don't lose control when you take a drink of water, so perhaps you don't need to lose control at the pool. "But it's a public pool!" you say. Yes, and the health department requires that pool owners maintain a "ten-second kill" with its sanitizing chemistry. (It won't hurt your tongue cells.) Everyone gets water in his mouth every once in a while. If the pool is a reputable one and if it's unsafe for any reason and the staff knows about it, you will be called out of the water.

As for letting water into your nose, it's no fun to let water into your nose on purpose. Let's just wait until it happens by accident and see if you can remain in control.

_____ I am not a floater.

What is a floater? A floater is someone who is supported by the water when he lies on it, whether his feet are at the surface or at the bottom in shallow water. To review, a sinker is a person who, when she fills her lungs maximally and then lies down on the water, goes to the bottom and doesn't float back up. To see if you're a floater, take that "test," if you can be in control for it.

_____ It would be unwise of me to relax in water.

Why would it be unwise? If you would panic, then yes, it would be unwise. Otherwise, test this belief by seeing what happens if you relax completely in very shallow water. You may need to use a nose clip or hold your nose.

_____ If I relax in water, I'll drop to the bottom like a stone.

Are you willing to relax in water and test this? Go to a comfortable depth to try it. If you think it would be different in deep water, you can test that later when you're ready. Start in shallow water. Remember, we don't care if you test it. We only care that you remain in control. If this isn't possible yet, then I trust you won't perform this test. Test the front float first. Wearing a tether helps but it's not essential.

_____ I am not a swimmer yet.

Do you think that just because you don't swim, or because you panic in deep water or you get water in your nose, or you can't open your eyes under water, or you sink, or you can't get a breath, or you never passed a swimming test, you weren't born a swimmer? *Impossible!*

When will you think of yourself as a swimmer? When you can dive into the pool and swim a length with easy breathing? When you can tread water, or swim from one place to another without panicking? When you can do X, Y, or Z? If so, that would mean that you believe in the sequence, "Have, Do, Be" instead of "Be, Do Have," discussed earlier.

Please consider this idea. Every human being is born a swimmer. You were born with the blueprint to learn to swim, just as you were born with a blueprint to read, drive, walk, and talk.

You were taught the steps of reading one by one. You started at the beginning, were given the steps, and mastered the skills so you could read with ease. With swimming, you may have been given steps out of order—and many of the most important steps were skipped. There was virtually no way to succeed with steps missing.

There *is* a swimmer within you. The light is on; the shade is simply pulled down. We are raising the shade so your swimmer-self can shine through, which it will surely do if you start at the beginning and skip no steps.

Given these ideas, can you accept, at least intellectually, that you were born a swimmer? If you can, you'll have made a small shift inside you. This shift at the level of your thoughts must ripple out to affect your experience.

_____ I have to push myself in order to learn to swim.

Have you tried anything besides pushing? What would happen if you didn't push—if you allowed yourself to be just where you are? You owe it to yourself to find out. When you do, it may be the first time you've been in the 1st Circle in the water.

_____ If I relax in water, I might lose control.

Can you go to very shallow water where you feel safe and see what happens if you relax? It's okay to leave your hands on the bottom. Or in a standard-depth pool, use a tether.

If you can't relax, can you feel the tension in your body and let it be there? Just allow it. If it becomes uncomfortable, stand up, sit up, or take a break. Then allow it some more.

_____ I may not have adequate lung capacity to swim.

You may need to test this one later—but if you have already swum (moved from here to there with ease), you can justifiably say that you have adequate lung capacity to swim. You may need to learn how to breathe as you swim.

_____ If I want to learn to swim, I have to follow instructors' directions even if I don't want to.

Hopefully this book is convincing you that you are your own boss when it comes to learning. Only you know what's needed to have fun.

_____ Each breath I take must be maximal in case I don't get another one.

Any breath you take is going to run out in a while. You're going to have to stand up to get another one, no matter what. So why not take a comfortable one? By the way, pushing yourself and fear use up your air sooner.

Once you know how to stop and stand up, you can get a breath whenever you want in shallow water. Once you know how to roll over on your back and float, staying in your body 100% of the time, you can get a breath whenever you want in shallow water and theoretically in deep water. It's only time to do this *if you can stay in your body for it.*

Perhaps you think you could do it, but you wish you had a spotter with you in the deep end. If so, you have reached a milestone: wanting to try it in the deep, believing you can stay in your body with a spotter. Take a moment to acknowledge yourself for this.

If no spotter is available, you can still make progress on your own. You could use a tether at the deep end ladder. Or, continue to practice rolling over on your back in shallow water. Rest on your back, making sure you are in shallow water where your body is. When you've done this enough, say, 100 times (but only you will know for sure), you'll be so convinced that you can remain in control any time you do it that you truly will be safe in the deep. Your body will notify you.

Then you can practice the roll-over in the shallow and visualize yourself being in the deep. I don't mean to leave your body in the shallow and go to the deep with your thoughts. I mean pretend, by closing your eyes, that you're doing your roll with 8 feet of water below you. Go slowly and stay in your body for it. When you're in control for this, you can ask a lifeguard to watch you practice it in the deep.

_____ To float correctly, my body should be horizontal.

Dispelling this belief requires an understanding of what "floating correctly" means. "Correctly" means the position you float in when you're doing zero work besides holding your breath (in a front float). Are you doing any work when you float? Find the correct float for you. If you resist a diagonal float for example, it will be stressful. If you let your body float in its natural position, you'll have a float that works and is restful. Use a nose clip, if need be, to remove any concern about water in your nose. The same things are true for the back float but it's not a requirement that you hold your breath.

_____ In order to rest, I need the bottom or the side.

Can you rest on your back? If you know the back float and you know how to roll from your stomach to your back, why not test resting on your back? See how long you can *not* stand up or hold the side, for fun. It may be just a few seconds. Notice the time. Even a few seconds is notable progress. If your feet go to the bottom in your float, rest that way; it still counts.

_____ The water is more powerful than I am.

Is it more powerful than you in a pool? At what point is it more powerful than you? Is it more powerful than you when you don't feel in control? Is it more powerful at any other time? If you're thinking about the ocean, there are times when it's more powerful than we are, but we usually don't go swimming at those times. If you get a surprise from the ocean, the safest you can be is to know how to stay in your body.

_____ I need to be more physically fit than I am to learn to swim.

To dispel this belief, you just need to experience moving from here to there in the water. It takes less energy than walking. You're on your way. If you are a generally healthy person, you do not need to be any more physically fit than you are now to swim. The process of learning to swim can be the activity that increases your fitness level. You may visualize huffing and puffing to get to the other side, but this characterizes a swimmer who doesn't know how to stay in his body. He doesn't know that the goal is to remain in control, not to get to the other side. There's no reason to get winded unless you want to, or unless you aren't paying attention to your comfort.

_____ Other shallow water beliefs that are operating (list them here):

_____

_____ This system may work for others, but it may not work for me.

To dispel this belief, you'll have to give this book and its steps a try. It has worked for everyone who has tried it since 1983: about 6000 people to date.

You can test any belief you have. I encourage you to test each one if you can do so safely. If something it too scary to test, break it into smaller parts.

DISPELLING YOUR UNWANTED DEEP-WATER BELIEFS

As you dispel your unwanted shallow water beliefs, a sweet thing happens. Your mind opens to the possibility that the same things may be true in deep water. You become curious to try them. You're right; the same things are true in deep water. Now you need to be able to stay in your body in deep water to experience them. This is a place where the tether comes in handy.

Being able to stay in your body comes from:
- Practicing staying in your body
- Practicing staying in your body for skills that you once left your body for, by doing them only to the point that you're comfortable—giving yourself full permission to go only this far, and then stop.
- Trusting and remaining in trust

_____ I don't trust myself in deep water.

You're building a groundwork (infrastructure) of trust in yourself that will expand to deep water if you start at the beginning and skip no steps.

Dispelling your deep-water beliefs is a work in progress, and you are progressing.

_____ Other deep-water beliefs you want to dispel:

_____

_____

How can you test those beliefs safely?

_____

_____

STEP 69: COMMON MISUNDERSTANDINGS

There are a few commonly heard phrases about swimming that are familiar to "everyone" that never should have been taken literally: they are not true. Let's get these straightened out now.

- "Your hands should be cupped when you swim."
- "Keep your knees straight when you kick."
- "You should be horizontal to float correctly."
- "If you're tense, you'll sink."

CUPPED HANDS: MISUNDERSTANDING

As explained earlier, the most efficient position of your hands when you pull yourself through the water is open and flat. The flatter the palm of your hand is, the larger the surface area is, and the more water you can push against.

Cupped hands are inefficient and require more work.

Her cupped hands hinder her somersault.

Straight Legs: Misunderstanding

Instructors who are heard to say, "Keep your legs straight when you kick," hopefully don't mean to keep them literally straight. They mean, "straight as compared to bending your knees at 90 degrees or more." If you were to keep your knees straight, you would get zero propulsion from your kick. You could even go backward.

The kick is outside the scope of this book. However, let's put the misunderstanding to rest. The maximum amount of bend in the knees recommended for the flutter kick is exceeded in the following photo:

This kick will move you. A bit less bend would be more effective.

Floating Horizontally: Misunderstanding

We have already established that it's not true that the only correct float is a horizontal one. Any position you float in is good.

IF YOU'RE TENSE YOU'LL SINK: MISUNDERSTANDING

Your body's ability to float depends on your body composition and your air. Your body composition and air don't change suddenly if you become tense. If your neck becomes tense in a back float and it pulls your chin and face below the surface, you'll just pull your chin and face below the surface: you won't sink.

You won't sink unless you have no buoyancy. Remember, some people can't sink even if they let out all their air.

> STUDENT MARSHA SAID, "WHEN INSTRUCTORS
> TOLD ME THAT IF I WAS TENSE, I'D SINK,
> I BECAME AFRAID TO BE AFRAID.

Try this if it sounds like fun. Go into a front float. Then tense up as much as you can. Notice that you don't even go one inch closer to the bottom. You remain floating, but tensely.

LADIES—"UGH, I HAVE TO REMOVE MY SUIT" MISUNDERSTANDING:

At the restroom, just pull the lowest edge of your suit to the side.

STEP 70: REVERSALS

Another skill that gives you more freedom in water is the reversal. In a reversal you go from a back float into a front float by almost standing up, but moving forward into a front float instead.

Lie on your back in a back float.

Remain still for a while, so that you're totally present in the back float, going nowhere. You're not planning ahead: you're in the present.

Comfortable back float. Notice how relaxed her fingers and feet are.

Then, begin to unfloat by picking up your head and drawing up your knees.

When you pick up your head, take a breath, since soon your face will be going into the water. After taking a breath, she pulls her knees toward her head, causing her to rotate.

Finish bringing your face and knees together so that your body is in a ball.

Then wait. You don't have to do anything with your arms or legs. In two or three seconds, the laws of physics will move you. Your body will begin to rotate forward. Instead of standing up, let yourself rotate all the way into your front float.

With no further movement of her limbs, she allows herself to continue rolling forward into a front float. She didn't put her hands out front: that's where they float.

You have reversed your direction and gone from back to front. This is handy if you want to float away from the wall on your back and return.

STEP 71: COMPARING YOURSELF TO OTHERS —REMINDER

If you find yourself saying, "She can do this better than I can," or "Everyone is learning faster than I am," or "I don't belong here," stop yourself for a moment and examine what you're doing. If there's no charge on your comments, fine (in other words, if your comments are made neutrally with no negativity attached).

Do you *want* to compare yourself to others? Will it help you reach your goals? Does it feel good?

When we compare ourselves to others, we are usually out of our bodies. We are over at theirs (or somewhere else) looking back at ours. That alone is enough to signal that we're making a mistake. If we're not in our bodies, we have lost our presence to what we were doing.

Obviously, it's perfectly okay to be out of your body if you're asleep, day-dreaming, looking objectively at yourself, or fantasizing something pleasant. It's an inno, however, if you're preventing yourself from being where you want to be.

When you learned to walk and talk, you went at the perfect pace for you. It was the pace that allowed you to find all the nuances of walking and talking, balance, posture, how to shape your mouth, how to form the words, etc., so that you could find your way successfully. In the end, you were perfectly good at walking and talking. If any step had been skipped, it would have taken longer to learn. Or you wouldn't have learned at all. But you learned beautifully.

Can you allow yourself to find your own way with swimming? See if the message of this book fits you. If you follow it, you won't skip any steps—you can only succeed. If you aren't following the steps, or you're skipping steps, then you can expect to have some difficulty and you may not learn. It simply doesn't get any more basic than staying comfortable: in your body.

If someone else is doing something that you can't do yet, does it mean anything? It may mean that they already learned something you haven't learned yet. Then it's not time for you to do what they're doing. You're not "behind." You're where you need to be in order to embody the step you're on. You'll naturally and effortlessly come to the next step.

If you say, "But I'm behind where I should be," you're saying there's a standard of performance that you're not living up to in your own mind. Do you know what learning to swim should look like?

You as a spirit are ahead of or behind your body. In other words, you're out of your body, not in the 1st Circle.

I'm behind..

We aren't in control of when we get there, anyway. Wouldn't it be more useful to let yourself off the hook? To stop pushing? To push on something, you have to be beside it. To push yourself, you have to be beside yourself, not in the 1st Circle.

You must be beside yourself to push yourself.
This is not where you want to be.

Instantly you know that to push yourself is incorrect. Yes, there is such a thing as pushing yourself from within, such as when you're in a race and you speed up to beat the person in front of you. But that's different.

Can you trust that by simply staying in your body you'll reach your goals in the shortest possible time? I hope so. It's true. Let yourself be where you are. It's the shortcut to your goals.

STEP 72: WHEN TO GO AND WHEN TO HOLD

Rule of thumb: if you're not sure whether you're ready to go on to the next step, you're not. When you've mastered something, you'll know. There will be no question in your mind. Then the next step will approach you.

If you've mastered something and you continue to practice it completely in the 1st Circle, a new thought or whim will cross your mind, a creative idea, which will usher you to a new experience. This is how you learned to walk, believe it or not. This is how you, a natural learner, keep learning without being taught. And this is why it's never necessary to push yourself in order to learn.

LEARNING LOOKS LIKE THIS: 5TH CIRCLE TO 1ST CIRCLE

As you know, the steps of going from calm to panic involve going from being in your body to leaving it altogether. It's a process of becoming less present until we have virtually no presence at all.

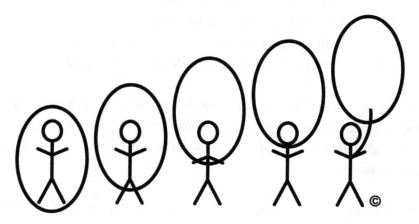

Losing control. The Steps of Panic. © M. Dash 1983.

The steps of learning are the exact opposite. They go from having no presence at all (no control) for the skill to being completely present doing it.

241

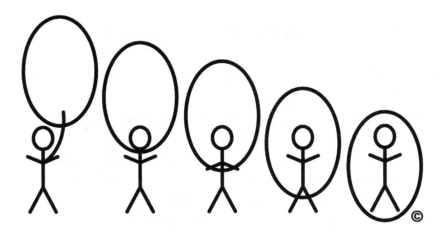

Gaining control. The Steps of Learning. © M. Dash 1984.

Before you learn something, there's no sense of connection to the information you want. As you learn, it seems that you bring new information into your mind.

But it's more useful to think of it like this. Your mind is in every cell of your *body*! When it feels as though you are bringing new information into your mind, you're actually bringing more *presence* into your *body*! So you learn as you become more present to your *body*. It tells you to stop, go, ask questions.

Observing my classes has taught me that information is everywhere. There's no spot where *all* information is not. The answer to every question that can be asked is right here and everywhere. It may not be known, but it's here. We just need to bring our presence to it.

Before learning, you have no sense of certain information: no connection to it:

No sense of connection to the information but you're listening

In the second stage of learning, you start to have a mental understanding of something, but you can't do it yet:

Beginnings of a mental understanding, a mental connection.

In the third stage, when you're starting to get it, you're further into your body:

Starting to get it: sometimes you can do it, sometimes you can't

In the fourth stage, when you've almost gotten it, but you know it's "not quite there yet," it looks like this:

Almost have it

In the fifth stage, when you've filled your body with presence down to your toes, you've "gotten it down"—embodied the skill or belief. You've learned it.

Got it down

We say, "I made the connection." When this connection is made, a circuit is closed, exactly like when an electrical circuit is closed and instantly a light bulb goes on.

As you learn the steps of each skill in this book, you close circuit after circuit. Suddenly you have the breathing. Suddenly you have freedom in the deep. You "get it." When you become fully present in the deep, you've learned to swim.

Out of your body, you can't learn; you can't connect with the information that's there. When you're present in your body, the information is "right there." You say, "It just came to me."

Though this happens at a different pace for everyone, the steps are universal. And they can only happen when we're in our bodies, connected to ourselves.

Given this model of learning, how far down into your body have you embodied the belief, "I'm safe in shallow water?" Draw a circle to show how far.

How far have you embodied the belief, "I'm safe in deep water"? Draw a circle below to show how far.

Does this way of thinking about learning make sense to you?

MASTERY

Remember when the first computers were made? They took up the space of an entire room. Today, a tiny chip can do the same amount of work.

Our minds work much the same way. When we first learn something, it requires all of our attention. There's no way you could be talking on the phone while you were learning how to walk a tightrope. There's no way we can learn two things at once, although it's attempted by many people daily. It just doesn't work. Go ahead and try to think of an example of learning two things at once. I suggest that either both went unlearned, or only one was actually learned. When you add the factor of fear for your life, you can easily see that "you must be present to learn."

When we allow ourselves to give our full attention to what we're learning, we learn beautifully. We ask our questions. They're answered. We go to the next level of understanding. We take the next risk because it's fun. We grow. Our presence becomes a habit. Skills become reliable.

Once we've learned something, the amount of attention required to do it is less than when we began to learn it. Let's say that once we learn it, we can do it with one quarter as much attention. It requires little attention—presence— to do a skill when we've learned it.

When we've mastered it, it's something we can do with almost no presence whatsoever. We can do it "on automatic." This is why people can use lap swimming as a form of meditation. They are far from (notice the location: far) having to think about their safety, their buoyancy, their stroke, or their breathing. They have mastered these things so that they can now "go" different places with their attention and thoughts.

The picture that we would add to the series of circles above is this:

MASTERY
The skill takes very little attention: very little of your presence.
It's represented by the small dot at the chest.

The small space that mastery takes up is not really located in your chest or in any one part of your body. This dot is simply a representation of the tiny space mastery takes up in each of your cells, relative to the larger amount of space needed when you have to put a lot of attention on something.

Just as your presence as a spirit is in every cell of your body, mastery is located in every cell of your body. This change in your cells—mastery—builds infrastructure.

THE IMPERATIVE OF STAYING IN YOUR BODY

How are you doing with the teaching in this book? Do you believe that it's more important to stay in your body at all costs than it is to learn a mechanical skill?

Let's review.

- In order to learn, you must feel safe.

- If you feel safe, you feel in control in the moment. You have your survival needs taken care of and you have attention to spare for something else.

- If you feel safe, you can learn.

- The reason you haven't learned in the past is that you didn't feel safe and you weren't in control.

- The "anatomy" of feeling safe and being in control is that you're in your body: you and your body are in the same space.

- The process of losing safety and losing control is movement of you from your body outward (out of your body).

- The way to prevent "losing it," that is, losing control or losing your presence of mind, is to stay comfortable. By staying comfortable, you keep yourself in your body on purpose.

- There are two optimum speeds: Slow and Stop. If you feel uncomfortable, stop. Wait until you feel comfortable again. Then go slowly. You can be in a race and still be slow on the inside.

- What you *feel* guides what you do next. Your feeling tells you when to stop. You don't need to know what to do later. You only need to know what to do now.

- If you feel yourself speeding up inside, your feeling is telling you that you're in danger. It may be only a belief, but you must honor it. It's telling you to slow down or stop so you can maintain control and stay safe.

- Every time you've learned something, you've been in your body. (Check to see if you can find any exceptions.)

- To guarantee your success in learning *anything*, you simply need to keep yourself in your body.

If you have reached this part of the book, and you haven't been in the water to master the topics and skills that have been covered, go back. Take your time. Don't push yourself. As you can see, pushing doesn't work with overcoming fear or learning. Don't you owe it to yourself to give yourself a chance? Allow yourself to be completely present for each part. Your body tells you when it's time to proceed.

STEP 73: JUMPING IN

Would you like to be able to run off the deck and jump into the deep end in a cannonball, like a kid? No? Fair enough. How about gently slipping into the pool off the edge? If you start at the beginning and skip no steps, it's inevitable that you'll be able to do either of these in a while. Let's start at the beginning.

In shallow water, chest deep or less, hop up and down.

- As you hop, notice what parts of your body are being used most: the balls of your feet, your thighs, knees, ankles and hips. As your weight comes down onto your feet and the bottom of the pool, your joints absorb most of the force. They make your landing soft on your body.

- As you hop, turn around a full 360 degrees. Notice that you don't need to be taught how to do this.

- Now hop, turning the other way.

- Now hop a little higher. When you hop higher, you'll land with a little more force on your feet. This requires that you bend your knees a little more to absorb your weight. It also requires that your other joints absorb a little more, too. Notice these changes. This is how you protect your body. When you jump into a pool, your joints will absorb a little *more* of your weight so that you land safely.

- Always land on your feet. Only when you jump from the deck into deep water (8-10 feet) would you *not land* on your feet—you probably wouldn't reach the bottom at all.

- When you've become accustomed to jumping higher, visualize yourself jumping up so high that you'd go under water when you landed in order to land softly. See yourself doing this a number of times.

- When you can see this in your mind and you're ready, try it. It doesn't matter whether you jump high or not: just practice landing as though you had. When you go under water, it's a good idea for now to use a nose clip or hold your nose.

- When you've done this many times, ask yourself if you're ready to try this from a sitting position on the side of the pool. If not, fine.

- If yes, sit on the deck at the edge. Put one hand on the edge and one on your nose. Give yourself a "scoot" off the deck and land on your feet gently, absorbing your weight with your joints. It's okay to leave one hand on the deck as you enter.

How did it go? Practice it 20 or 30 times over your next few pool visits.

STEP 74: GETTING OUT OF THE POOL

There's the obvious way out of the pool using the ladder or steps. Then there's jumping out, which is sometimes more convenient. This takes a few practices to make it smooth (making it one of the quickest things to learn), but it may take doing it a 10 times in a week to gain the strength for it. The strength comes surprisingly soon if you stick with it for a few days.

Climbing out of the pool without the ladder

1. Place your hands on the deck or the gutter ready to spring.
2. Jump up, press down on the deck or gutter, and straighten your elbows.
3. Put your knee on the deck or gutter and climb up.

MILESTONE

At this point, you've covered all the basic skills in shallow water that enable you to play and explore in shallow water safely. The most important of these skills is staying in your body. You've covered them: now take time to master them. Give yourself a standing ovation! Take a break and absorb this victory!

When you've done that, you can take yourself and your new infrastructure to the deep end. If you wish to visit the deep end before you've mastered the shallow end skills, please do what's fun.

STEP 75: DEEP WATER

As one student said,

Deep water is more fun now. Shallow water is boring. —Ram

It's possible to learn to be comfortable in deep water without ever going into it. It's a perfectly good way to become 100% calm about deep water. You won't be able to show anyone that you're in control if you don't have a deep end, but you can know this beyond a shadow of a doubt for yourself. Do you believe this?

To do that, practice the front and back floats in the shallow water until you've become so anchored in your body and you've tested the water's buoyant force so many times and in so many positions that you've convinced yourself that it's reliable and it's never going to change. This would be some (more) of the most worthwhile time you have ever spent in your life, I daresay. Though I have only given one paragraph to that suggestion, I could end the book here. It truly is a worthy pursuit.

This is the best thing I've ever done. —Many students

If you have a deep end at your pool, then, if and when your curiosity gets the best of you and there's someone else at the pool to check on you, head for the deep. Holding onto the gutter/wall, make your way slowly, hand over hand, toward the deep water. As you go, check in with yourself. Am I in my body? Is this fun? Stop and regroup if you get ahead of yourself. Stop and stay at the depth where you can be comfortable while still holding on.

Ahead of yourself   **Comfortable**

No pushing. If you're in control and having fun, it's only a matter of *when* you want to go to the deep end, not "if." The time will come. But if you're never ready, that's okay, too.

> WE DON'T CARE IF YOU GO INTO THE DEEP END.
> WE ONLY CARE THAT YOU FEEL IN CONTROL
> AND ARE HAVING FUN.

Remember what Student Sylvia said:

> *If I know I can't put my feet on the bottom, I panic. I can fake it for a while, but then the truth comes and gets me.*

She knew it wasn't time to go to the deep end yet; she couldn't remain in control.

When you have gone as far as it's fun toward the deep end, stop and feel your feelings. Are you totally calm? Great! Would you like to rest here for a while? Put your face in? Just have fun.

Or, is your heart beating faster than normal? Is there any tension in your body? These are both okay, as long as you're still having one of the two kinds of fun.

Let your heart beat any way it wants to beat. Let any tension be there. Is it in your hands? Your arms? Your gut? Just feel it and allow it. Stay there as long as you're curious about it. If it's not okay, go back toward the shallow end; it's not time to be in the deep. Go back and practice things that are comfortable in the shallow end. Call it a successful day.

If you have the tether for the deep end, you can have a different experience of safety and experimenting like a kid.

2+2=4
IT'S OKAY NOT TO BE READY TO LEARN IN THE DEEP END.

Why Return to the Shallow End to Practice Something I'm Already Comfortable Doing?

Remember: it's useful to practice something you're already comfortable doing because you can still bring more of your presence to it (unless you've mastered it). This was discussed in Step 77. Therefore, if you go back to the shallow end, you can still make progress. The fun you have will either teach you or heal you. If it's not fun, don't do it.

If you decide to remain in the deep end, what, if anything, feels different about being in the deep? Often people say, "I can't feel the bottom," or "I feel more buoyant." What do *you* feel?

Make an agreement with yourself now. Promise, I *will not let go of the wall today in the deep end.* That's just for now. Agreed? We want you to feel safe and to know you can stay in control.

Alternatively, use the tether to connect to a rung of the deep end ladder. Play.

Step 76: Feeling Deep Water Hold You Up on Your Front

If it sounds like fun, keeping your grasp of the wall in the deep end, lower your face into the water and let your body dangle. Let the water support you. Your hands will prevent you from drifting away. But they shouldn't support you; the water will. You won't kick your feet up behind you, right? Because you know that letting your feet go where they naturally go is the best way to find your natural float.

How does it feel? Does it feel the same as your float in shallow water, or different?

Spend some time in this float, coming up to rest whenever you want. Is there any tension as you float? Let it be there. What happens?

Right, it disappears. If it hasn't disappeared, then guess what? You must be in a hurry, or you're pushing yourself a bit or an old belief is showing. Remember, it's okay to go back to shallow water if being in the deep isn't fun.

Give yourself many minutes over several days to feel the deep water holding you up. It takes a while for most people to believe it. You want to believe it in your gut. You want to embody the belief that you float in deep water. Prove it to yourself, without letting go of the wall if you don't have the tether.

You probably want to know if the float will work if you let go as well. There will be a time soon when you can experiment with that. One way to test it is to put your clasped hands behind the ladder's side-rail and feel yourself float.

The certainty that deep water holds you up just as shallow water does is a knowing that you have probably sought for a long time. *Give yourself time to absorb this.*

IF YOU FEEL MORE BUOYANT IN DEEP WATER THAN IN SHALLOW

Often people report feeling more buoyant in the deep water than in the shallow. How can this be? The water's density is not different between the shallow and deep. Your body's density isn't different between shallow and deep. So the relationship between the two densities isn't different, either. Therefore, physics says your buoyancy is exactly the same in both shallow and deep. Yet people commonly *feel* more buoyant in the deep.

If you're in the shallow end, you're always aware of the bottom. You always know it's there if you want it. If you're always aware of it, some of your presence is always there. Some of *you* is at the bottom. The rest of you is at the top. You're split. The two parts of you pull to be together, like magnets.

You and your body are in two places. You feel a pull toward the bottom.

If you feel pulled by the bottom, it's because so much of your attention is on the bottom.

If you feel more buoyant in the deep end, it's because you're not depending on the bottom to stand up or rest. You've let go of using it. This letting go allows you to be fully at the surface with your body. With you and your body at the top, you feel lighter and more buoyant.

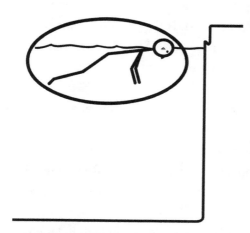

Feeling buoyant in the deep: you and your body are together.
Eventually, you'll also disconnect from the bottom in the shallow.

Step 77: Ladder Game

How far down into your body have you embodied the belief, "Deep water holds me up?" Go to the deep-end ladder *if it sounds like fun*. Keeping yourself vertical, *take a breath* and climb down the ladder as far as you would like to go. Look straight ahead—don't look up. This protects your nose. If your feet start to float up behind you, it's okay: you forgot to stay vertical. The game will still work. If you want to stay vertical, you'll have to adjust your alignment and posture to keep your feet directly under you as you descend. Go slowly and feel what you have to do to stay vertical. See how far you can have fun descending.

We don't care if you go down the ladder even one rung. We only care that you remain in control and have fun.

You may have to work to descend! When you have descended as far as you're comfortable, you may feel pressure on your ears. This is normal. The deeper you go, the more pressure there is on any air space in your body. Your ears are the place you feel it most. If the pressure bothers you, come back up the ladder a rung or two to relieve it. If you have a cold, or are getting one, you may feel it at only 2 or 3 feet of depth.

On the other hand, you may feel no pressure at all, even at ten feet.

When you're as deep as you want to go on the ladder, try this test. Remember: we don't care if you do this—only that you feel completely in control and are having fun.

Loosen your grip on the ladder, but not enough to let go of it completely (unless you'd like to). Expect that the water will push you back to the surface as though you're on an elevator. It's a free ride. They say there's no "free ride," but they didn't think about deep water. It's always a free ride up from under water if you're buoyant.

Be a kid. Take this ride a hundred times. "Watch me, Mom!" Prove to yourself that the water pushes you up when you have air. Isn't this something you want to know? Give yourself time to embody this truth. It may take a few days. Be considerate of others who may want to exit and enter the pool at the ladder. Remember, while you're below the surface, protect your nose by looking straight ahead or downward, not up.

STEP 78: VERTICAL FLOAT

At the ladder, if it's not getting too much use by others, experiment with keeping your body floating in a vertical position. Hold onto the ladder.

Floating vertically is a first step toward bigger things that shall remain nameless for now. Start by taking a breath and holding it, as always. To float straight up and down you'll have to keep your body aligned, head above spine, spine above hips, and hips above knees. If your head is tilted forward, you'll tip forward into a front float. If it's tilted backward, you'll go into a back float. Line yourself up vertically at the ladder or wall and see if you can balance as though you were standing on the water.

- Keep your hands on the side rails of ladder but let the water hold you up.
- Align your head directly above your spine.
- Keep your feet from going up behind you (or ahead of you) by keeping your thighs and knees below your spine. It takes some balancing.

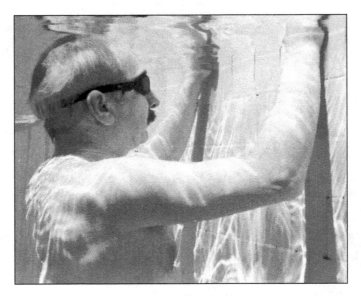

Getting ready for a vertical float.
He's making sure that the water is holding him up, not his hands.

Below, vertical floats in the deep:

She knows that the water will hold her up, so she's comfortable with her arms at her sides. She aligns herself vertically.

Vertical float, midpool. Aligned from head to foot.

If you find yourself tipping forward or backward, feel whether you're letting your head drop forward or backward.

Head tipped forward leads to a front float.

Your front float may be more horizontal than this. If your head were tipped backward, you'd move to a back float.

One of the first things you'll notice as you experiment is that you don't sink. *You remain afloat.* Yes, you. There you are, the top of your head and perhaps even some of your forehead or face, out of the water. The more air you have and the more buoyancy you have, the higher you'll float. Spend some time with this new feeling in deep water. Let it sink in. Part of learning is being pleasantly surprised, marveling at how this could possibly be true after all these years of thinking otherwise, reveling in the wonder of the truth, and watching your expectation of what will happen next time change to what really happens. You're getting the picture! This is an example of moving your foot from one rung on the ladder *toward* the next one. A lot is happening here.

Reminder: if you're in a vertical float and your nose is below the water, don't tip your head back unless you're wearing a nose clip (or you blip)—you'll get water in your nose.

VERTICAL FLOAT IF YOU'RE A SINKER

If you're a sinker, you won't be able to stay at the surface for the previous exercise. To make yourself as buoyant as you can be (which is not buoyant), take the maximum amount of air you can comfortably hold. Remember, being a sinker is not a problem. It just means you'll learn to stay afloat by other means. The means are coming soon. Only experiment in deep water if you know you can be in control of coming back up.

For a sinker, the exercise above is about taking a good breath and allowing yourself to sink. You can do this in water that's 6 feet deep if you want to be able to stand on the bottom and reach the deck. Or, you can sink all the way to the bottom in the deep end. Someone should be watching you as you experiment with this. They should have a pole to extend to you in case you need assistance there at the bottom. But you and I know (right?) that you wouldn't try something that you can't be in control for.

Alternatively, in deep water, you can stop your sinking by holding onto the ladder at the depth you want to stop. Or use a tether. Do what's comfortable for you. You can bring yourself back up the ladder at any time. Monitor your air so you feel safe. Come up while you still have plenty of air.

Go down the ladder or to the bottom many times. Remember, we only care that you feel 100% in control and safe.

Sinkers can jump off the bottom to go up. You can use your arm sweep to swim back to the surface, too.

If it sounds like fun, once you're on the bottom and feeling safe, take a moment to look around. Check out the view. The world looks different from the bottom of the deep end. Few people in all of humanity have seen it. Don't look up unless your nose is protected.

STEP 79: FEELING DEEP WATER HOLD YOU UP ON YOUR BACK

In the shallow end first, and then in the deep, review the exercises that remind you that deep water holds you up. Each time you go to the deep end, it pays to review this feeling and anchor it further into your body until you believe it.

To feel the water hold you up on your back, hold onto the deep end wall again and let your body be flush with the wall. Your chest, stomach, thighs, and toes will all be touching it.

Begin this way:

Remember: keep your body flush against the wall.

Lean back a bit and lower yourself down into the water so that your ears are in. Don't let go of the wall. Let yourself be completely supported by the water, not by your hands. The water will hold you up (unless you're a sinker). Your hands simply keep you from drifting away.

Remember, do this...   **...not this.**

Now, take a breath and hold it. What happens? Now let your air out. What happens?

Take a comfortable breath and hold it. Keep your hands on the wall. Can you feel the float? Practice back floating at the wall and become comfortable with it. You can also do this with the tether.

If you'd like to try breathing in a back float, notice that as you breathe, your floating level changes, as it did in the shallow end. If you inhale, you rise. If you exhale, you drop. If you exhale too much, you could go below the surface if you aren't paying attention. But I know you are paying attention, so you prevented yourself from going somewhere you would be uncomfortable (under water on your back where you would get a snootfull if you weren't wearing a nose clip).

To float for a while in a back float with your hands on the wall like this, you need to find a level of air-exchange that allows you to stay at a comfortable "altitude." See what works.

If you're very buoyant, you can breathe normally, and your altitude will remain comfortable. If you aren't very buoyant, you may need to hold all your air in your lungs in order to float. There's something you can do to make up for this.

Step 80: For Sinkers, There's Sculling

If you're a sinker, or if you're not very buoyant and you float vertically only with a maximal breath, go to a depth where you feel 100% safe—four feet? Then, go into a back "float," (or "back sink") such as it is. Wear a nose clip. You'll need to hold as much air as you can. Your feet will be on the bottom, of course.

If you're fighting the fact that your feet are at the bottom, feel how much energy you're using to fight the natural laws. It's not time to learn sculling yet (defined in a few paragraphs). It's time to lie in the water diagonally or vertically with your feet on the bottom and fight the fact that you're lean. Or, sink all the way to the bottom and fight, resist and complain. Try to force your legs to float. Give it a go!

When you're satisfied that nothing you do will beat physics, take a humble moment to acknowledge surrender. It's okay to be lean. You can still be a good swimmer. Do you believe this? It will take just a little learning which teaches you more about how the water works, which everyone needs to know.

Allow your feet to be on the bottom, without any resistance. When you can do this, even though you will sink to the bottom on your back, you'll be in the 1st Circle for the first time with a back sink. After you fully and unequivocally accept this, you can learn how to stay up.

Yes, you can learn to stay up. Sculling is a movement you make with your arms and hands that gives your body lift in the water, whether or not you're buoyant. If you use it during a back float, it will prevent you from going below the surface even if you're a sinker. Remember, the Olympians need to stay up somehow when they're not swimming from here to there. This is how they do it.

When you're in a back float...

- if you push downward, where will that take you? _____

- if you push upward, where will that take you? _____

- if you push backward (toward your head), where will that take you?
  _____

- if you push forward (toward your feet), where will that take you?
  _____

In the water, you'll find that:

- pushing downward takes you up

- pushing upward takes you down

- pushing backward takes you forward

- pushing forward takes you backward

- pushing downward gives you the lift you need to reach the surface, but the lift is only temporary if you're a sinker. It disappears after the downward push. To stay afloat if you're a sinker, you need a movement that delivers constant lift.

In shallow water, go into your back sink wearing a nose clip. Before you drop below the surface, sweep your arms back and forth from the 3:00 and 9:00 positions (on the clock) to 6:00 and back to 3:00 and 9:00. (Your head is at 12:00.) Turn your wrists at the end of each sweep so that you're always pushing on the water with your pancake palms. Remember, your palms are your power surface.

A sinker on his way to sculling. He's almost there: his hands
need to be pitched downward more in order to get the lift he
needs. See photos below for correct hand angles.

An angle of about 30 degrees gives you lift when your palms sweep
sideways on the water (in this case, as she sweeps to our right).

Back and forth: pitch your hands like this.
The slight cupping in his left hand makes that hand less effective.

Good pitch for hands while sculling. This pitch, used while she sweeps back
and forth in her back float, will keep her up. Her palms could be flatter.

If you keep your hands pitched at the correct angle, about 30 degrees, you'll be able to keep yourself from sinking. Bingo.

How does it work? To get lift, you need to create at least a little downward force all the time. You create this by pitching your hands, as above. In each horizontal sweep of your arms—because the effect of your pitched palms causes pressure both sideways and downward and the movement of your palms is constant—you'll get constant downward force, and therefore, constant lift. This will keep you in a back float position where you can breathe and rest.

If you pushed your hands toward the bottom of the pool, it would give you lift as you pushed down, but when you raised your hands back up to prepare to push down again, you'd lose your lift.

Practice this every day you go to the pool, once you've reached this level of comfort. If you focus on staying in your body, feeling the pressure on your palms, you'll improve your lift every day.

Troubleshooting Sculling

What if your hands were vertical, as in the photo below? If they pushed and pulled, pitched at 90 degrees, they would give you zero lift: there would be no downward force.

What not to do. At 90 degrees, the hand pushes only sideways on the water: no lift. Additionally, her thumb position is keeping her palm from being flat.

If you hold your hands horizontally so that they slide through the water sideways without getting any purchase on it at all, this too will give you no lift.

Sliding the edges of your hand through the water gives you no lift, either.

The best hand angle is different for each person. Experiment to see what keeps you up for a second or two.

STEP 81: THE CONTROL METER

To what degree are you in control in shallow water? Rate your level of control on the Control Meter.

Control Meter
Are you 50% in control in shallow water? 100%?

What percentage of time are you completely in control in shallow water? _____ In deep water? _____

Each lesson in this book is about being in control. You can imagine a meter that measures your control level for each thing you do in the water, whether it's walking across the pool, lying on your back holding onto the wall, or letting go in deep water. One hundred percent control is mastery—the embodiment of control and peacefulness.

Only do those things that allow you to be in control all the time in the water. Make sure you're having fun!

> WHEN OVERCOMING FEAR, IT'S MORE ADVANCED
> TO REMAIN IN CONTROL AND ABORT A SKILL THAN
> TO COMPLETE THE SKILL AND LOSE CONTROL.

Your Learning

As we saw at the Learning Meter (Step 52), the quality of the learning can be very high if our questions are answered and we're given steps that meet us exactly where we are. We are able to make progress and feel successful. This is good learning (and teaching). On the other hand, if we're consistently given steps that are too advanced or too elementary for us, or we don't get correct answers to our questions, we are not being met at our level, and learning quality is low.

There are several components of learning. They're listed in the table below. Depending on what happens with each of these components, your learning quality will vary. Why discuss this? So that you know a good class from one that's not going to work so well.

Once you're aware of the information in the table, you can make an informed choice about classes that are suitable for you.

LEARNING QUALITY TABLE

LEARNING COMPONENT	LEARNING QUALITY		
	Low	Medium	High to Mastery
Feeling	Tension	Ease	Oneness with water
Internal Speed Or Frequency	High speed. High frequency.	Low speed. Low frequency.	Stillness
Presence	2nd to 5th circles	1st circle most of the time	Full presence for X; could do Y at the same time
Necessity of Returning to Your Body	High. Must return often.	Low. Can return when needed.	Very low. Can return when needed.
Physical Skills	Performed fast and with tension	Performed more slowly with little tension	Performed slowly, with ease, efficiency
Level of Fun	Not fun. Pushing, Frustration, self-doubt.	Willing. Fun most of the time.	Play. Joy. Can be meditative.

©Melon Dash 2005

Progression of learning quality from low to high over six learning components.

STEP 82: PLAY

Why are games and toys not only important, but necessary? During games and toys, you build confidence in yourself in various unpredictable situations. As you learn how to stay in your body, you learn how to be safe and in control. You learn about balance, about what the water does for you and what you must do for yourself. You develop a new relationship with water. It sparks your curiosity and brings new realizations.

If you've ever tried to put together the breath, float, arm stroke, and kick, it most likely didn't work. It may not have worked because:
- you probably weren't in your body
- you probably weren't in your body for any two of them at once
- you didn't have an understanding of how the water and your body work together
- you didn't believe the water would hold you up
- you were worried about your safety

Experimenting at your own level of confidence is fun. Finding the answers to your questions is fun. By following what's fun, you expand your understanding of the water. By practicing being in your body, your actions become organized: you bring your *whole being* to the table. When you have these two components under your belt—having fun and being in your body—you learn to swim.

GAME: POSITIONS

In shallow water, create and get into five new positions in the water that you could not accomplish on land. Use a nose clip.

DO WE CARE IF YOU GET INTO FIVE POSITIONS? NO.
WE ONLY CARE THAT YOU STAY IN
YOUR BODY AND HAVE FUN.

STEP 83: CHECK IN

How are you doing? Do you understand everything so far? Have you done the exercises? Are you finishing the book so you can go back and do the exercises?

If you follow your desire and do what's fun, no matter what it is, you'll learn in the best way. My two hopes are that you won't skip any steps and that if you have a question, you'll get the answer: either look back in the book (use the index), experiment, or, last gasp—send in a question.

If you find yourself feeling far better in the water than you ever have before, you may conclude that you're "there"—and you may be. You've made vast improvements. Check for full comfort: sometimes a student who says he feels fine is still tense. He feels fine in comparison to how he felt in the past. But compared to how calm he could feel, he still has a way to go. Just check your feelings and get your body's feedback. If you're calm, you know it.

THE NECESSITY OF REST

It goes without saying that when you get enough rest, you function best. When you're rested and present, you can feel "hunches." You can notice new ideas when they bubble up. You have time to consider them and follow up.

If you go, go, go all the time without stopping, you deny yourself natural shortcuts that are yours for the taking but which can't get through to you when your mind is too busy. When you stop, you're more receptive. Rest often as you learn. Resting reboots your presence.

At the pool, do what's fun. Make it easy for yourself.
You'll learn beautifully.

STEP 84: IF YOU'RE FEELING STUCK

Our natural rhythm is to expand and contract, expand and contract. We naturally expand when we're patient with ourselves, trust, go slowly and stay true to ourselves. Feeling "stuck" is a contraction. There's nothing wrong with contraction. But it doesn't feel good. If you feel stuck, knowing what it's about can help you to expand again. A contraction comes when a belief we have, whether we're conscious of it or not, stands in the way of expansion.

If you're feeling stuck, check to see if you're using the laws of learning favorably:
- Are you having fun?
- Are you practicing a skill rather than comfort?
- Are you pushing yourself?
- Are you practicing while frustrated?
- As you practice, are you "speeding" inside?
- Are you practicing while you're feeling any concern, worry, or fear?
- Have you asked for a spotter when you wanted one? (If one is not available, it doesn't mean you can't make progress.)
- Do you have a tether? It can replace a spotter if you proceed slowly.
- Do you have a question that hasn't been asked?
- Is there a nagging thought that hasn't been addressed?
- Are you criticizing yourself? Comparing yourself to others?
- Do you agree with the laws of learning taught in this book?

The resolution of each of these questions brings you back into your body. You can only learn while you're in your body.
- If you're not having fun, what *would be* fun?
- If you're practicing a skill, are you willing to practice comfort instead?
- If you're pushing yourself, are you willing to let yourself be where you are?
- If you're speeding, can you allow yourself to speed?
- If you're practicing frustration, would you change the subject or go "backward?"

- If you have a concern or worry, have you asked for help?
- If you have a question, will you ask it of someone who knows the answer?
- If there's a nagging thought, will you voice it?
- Will you give yourself a tether?
- Do you feel safe to speak up?
- If you're criticizing yourself or comparing yourself to others, you're outside of your body, looking back from another place. Are you willing to come back to your body and feel?

In this book you're relearning a way to learn. If it doesn't feel like your way, use what you can and leave the rest. The important thing is comfort.

Step 85: Breath Practice

Let's review breathing. Go to the shallow end of the pool. Hold onto the wall with one or both hands if it will make you more comfortable. Notice your breath for one minute. Notice the duration of your inhalation and the duration of your exhalation. Are they the same? Notice whether you're breathing through your nose or mouth.

Visualize yourself inhaling through your mouth and exhaling into the water through your nose. The inhalation begins, obviously, while you're standing up. The exhalation begins before your face goes into the water. It continues as long as you have plenty of air. It ends as you come back above the surface, exhaling the end of your breath into the air just before you take a new breath. Keep it comfortable. There should be no strain. When you feel the exhalation complete itself, take your new breath. You would not want to take a new breath before the old one was out; that would cause you to become winded. When you can imagine yourself doing this, go ahead and do it. Go slowly.

You have more air to exhale than you think. Don't push yourself with breathing. It has to feel safe and comfortable.

DO WE CARE IF YOU EXHALE INTO
THE WATER AND INHALE AS ABOVE?
NO. WE ONLY CARE THAT YOU FEEL IN CONTROL.

Remember, if your breath gets stuck (it stops coming out) or if you swallow, let it happen. Don't try to change it. You're getting into your body little by little and you need to let these things happen. Trust it. Give yourself time. This is an exercise to return to until your breathing is smooth and easy for minutes at a time.

STEP 86: SWIM STOP SWIM

This exercise is unrelated to the breathing exercise above.

In the shallow water, starting in your comfortable front float, practice swimming a few strokes as you hold your breath. Stand up when you need air. Do this a number of times, so it feels natural and familiar again.

Do it again, but this time, after you've swum a couple of strokes, stop everything. Let your body find its equilibrium position—the position it ends up in when you do nothing. It may take 5 seconds or so for your body to find equilibrium. Are you comfortable with the amount of air you took?

Your body may reach equilibrium in a horizontal position. It may reach equilibrium in a diagonal or vertical position. Give it time to get there.

After you have rested in equilibrium for a few seconds, resume swimming. Simply reach out front again and use your arm sweep to propel you forward. Feel your palms, as you sweep. These are your main points of connection with the water for propulsion. Yes, the inside surface of your arms also press on the water, but it's your palms' effect that is most powerful.

This exercise is about balance and control. Your balance changes when you stop, and you'll want to feel it. It seems like a small thing, but it's important. Everything in this book contributes to advancing one of the fronts. And that leads to closing the circuit of learning to swim.

Step 87: Approaching the Wall

Often when students swim toward the wall, they feel hurried as they approach, and grab it. They're so glad to get there! Have you felt this?

The cause of this is usually that the swimmer reaches the wall before her body arrives. She is ahead of her body. To cure this, as you swim toward the wall, keep yourself back where your body is. This means *feel* as you swim. Go slowly and stay in your body. Enjoy the whole ride. No beating your body to the wall. When you reach the wall, you'll be able to calmly put your hand up to it rather than grabbing it.

Step 88: Skipping Time

Let's talk more about swimming toward the wall and finding yourself scrambling to grab it. Let's talk about any time you feel yourself speeding up inside at the pool.

When this happens, there's a point at which something gets too scary and you start to "go away." The skill falls apart. When it's apart, it's uncomfortable and you stop. This allows you to return to safety. When you return to safety, you and your body come together again.

You left and the skill fell apart. You caught yourself (stopped) and your body caught up with you again. Take note: *you* move before your body does.

It's working.

It fell apart.

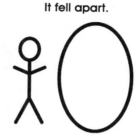

What fell apart? Connection with your body.

It wasn't the skill that got away from you. It was *you* that got away from you.

It fell apart.

I regrouped.

When you leave your body like that, you aren't in control of what's happening. You miss a few milliseconds. Though someone on the deck might be able to describe what you did, you can't. You might say, "I don't know what happened. It happened too fast."

You didn't skip time on purpose. This is the uncomfortable part. You can prevent this from happening.

To take the mystery out of a skill, do it in slow motion. Be willing to stop. Move so slowly that you're able to stay in your body to experience every millisecond.

If there's a part of the skill that's too scary to experience, *don't do it*. Only proceed as far as you're completely comfortable. Before it starts to get uncomfortable, stop. No kidding. We don't care if you do the skill. We only care that you feel in control. You're becoming an expert at staying in control. You will learn the skill, but not if you leave.

When you practice only the comfortable part over and over, feeling it as you practice, you bring more and more presence into your body. After a while, you have so much presence that you *want to continue the skill*. Now you can easily remain in your body for the next part of it, the part you had to leave for earlier. This is another law of learning:

> IF YOU PRACTICE A COMFORTABLE STEP WITH
> FULL PRESENCE, YOU WILL REACH
> THE NEXT STEP ORGANICALLY AND EFFORTLESSLY.

STEP 89: THE WHEEL

If you ever find yourself practicing a skill over and over again and having to abort it at the same point every time, it's because you're skipping time at that point. When you skip time at the same point every time, I call it being on The Wheel.

Your practice goes something like this. Let's use the back float as an example.
- You begin. You lie on your back.
- You feel the water holding you up.
- You float for few seconds and think to yourself, "Here I am in my back float—it's working."
- After a few more seconds, you say to yourself, "Hmm. I've been here for a while. I wonder how long this will last."
- Then something happens and before you know it, you're standing up.
- Now you're back at the beginning.
- You get ready to practice again. You're not sure what made you stop or how to make it work this time, but you're going to try.

You go around and around this wheel until you get frustrated or you get a new idea. You can have more control over it than that.

Do the skill again, and go slowly, feeling as you go, doing only what's comfortable. Let's get specific.

Choose a skill where you find yourself on The Wheel. Write down what happens at each of the five points above on The Wheel. Follow the example of the back float above.

The Wheel

Now, do the skill again. When you reach the point in the skill just before it usually falls apart, slow down and feel. Stay right there.

Any thoughts?

_____

_____

_____

Do it again. Stop while you're still comfortable. Remember, it's more advanced to abort a skill than to continue and leave the 1st Circle.

CONFIDENCE THAT'S NOT QUITE RIPE

Margaret practiced a skill so many times that she became confident. Then she did it one more time and something went wrong. She lost it and flew out of her body to the 5th Circle. This left a psychic dent, to say the least.

> *I was swimming from the deep end of the pool to the shallow end, got cold, started shivering, and panicked. Fortunately, Dennis was right there to push me toward the edge of the pool. I can't tell you how many times I have swum from one end of the pool to the other. But not this time.*

She and I discussed how to prevent this from happening again. This illustration is not about the distance or the deep water; it can be applied to any situation where confidence is not quite ripe.

Margaret was not 100% in her body during that lap. She thought she had it down and that she didn't have to go as slowly as she had in the beginning. But she hadn't fully learned the skill of staying present yet. Perhaps she had mastered it 75%.

If she had mastered being in her body, she would have been very sensitive to the nuances of feeling cold, her balance, breath, buoyancy, air supply, and ability to propel herself. She would have noticed some discomfort creeping in and made a correction to stop, regroup, and continue or rest. But since she hadn't mastered it yet, she was still vulnerable and had a moment when she scared herself.

You hit the nail on the head. I was definitely over-confident, not in my body or feeling. I recognize now that because of my over-confidence I did not take the time to feel before lift-off. I started to leave my body when I realized my legs were shaking so hard they were useless and that I was listing to one side, toward the middle of the pool rather than toward the shallow end. The interesting part was I kept thinking I would be okay but just needed some help. I did not even grab for Dennis. In the past I would have wrapped my arms around him in a death grip and nearly drowned both of us. I have not gone back into the deep end but have been enjoying the shallow end, doing things that are very comfortable and enjoyable. The interesting part is I feel as though I am developing new skills without trying.

What circles would you say Margaret went to? I'd say she started in the 2nd Circle, moved into the 3rd when she realized she was shaking, and had a moment of being in the 5th. Then Dennis pushed her to the side. In the past, when she put "a death grip on Dennis," it was an example of going out to the 5th Circle. It took her a few months and some good conversations to fully heal from the episode above. Margaret is now one of our expert spotters.

Step 90: What to Do If You Scare Yourself

If you scare yourself, you'll want a system that will help you recover and return to trust again.

If you scare yourself, there must have been some milliseconds when you and your body separated. You went out to the 5th circle and came back. It was not fun.

You may not have realized that you had a chance to prevent your "departure." Were there any signals your body was giving you that you either didn't feel because you were *thinking*, or that you dismissed?

Go over what happened in your mind. Do you remember the thoughts just before you lost control?

_____

_____

_____

Most likely, your thoughts took you out of the present moment. You were no longer feeling what was working for you—that the water was holding you up, or that you still had enough air to survive, or that you could safely swim to the side or stand up. Did your body give you any signals?

_____

_____

At what point in your thought process did you leave your body?

_____

_____

Do you remember how you got yourself out of this?

_____

_____

Then notice that you survived it. At least compliment yourself for that. But now you want to know how to prevent it from happening again.

Did you leave because it looked as though it was going to feel so bad that you didn't want to feel it?

_____

Did you leave because you forgot to go slowly? To "stay here"?

_____

I offer this: you left because you're still learning how not to leave. You're still learning that there's a more comfortable alternative to leaving. You haven't quite gotten it down yet, so you reverted back to an old habit. You made an inno. It's okay.

Is it okay with you? If it's not, write it out. Talk with someone who will just listen and not try to fix you. You can work through this if you can just talk it through, using what you're learning.

This is a moment of choice for you: do you want to hold this inno against yourself, or do you want to forgive yourself for it? Do you want to work toward mastery or maintain the pattern? There is no wrong answer.

If you want to give yourself the best chance of preventing this episode from recurring, understand how it happened and forgive yourself for it. It wasn't your fault. If you let yourself off the hook, you'll feel a physical letting go.

You may need to work through this a few times using the process given earlier. It's worth it, whatever time it takes. This is what "getting back on the horse" is really about. Getting back on the horse does not count if you aren't in your body. If you go about it correctly, you will heal your fear.

STEP 91: YOU

THE GRACEFUL, PATIENT ARTIST

There is enjoying yourself, taking things slowly and letting them unfold on their own. This is trust.

There's enjoying yourself, taking things slowly, letting them unfold as they do on their own, seeing some things succeed beautifully and others "fail," yet staying calm and continuing to trust. This is grace.

There's the slow passing of time with no apparent advance, which lies between a belief you've held for a long time and an awaited new understanding. There's the trust that this period of confusion will clear, and the answer will be known. This is patience.

There's the euphoria of unexpectedly experiencing a miracle. This is the glorious, yet predictable reward for enjoying yourself, taking it slowly, and letting things unfold as they do on their own. This is living artfully.

Recall that part of you that has lived artfully at times in your life, even in moments today. You are no stranger to living artfully. The real you is the artist. The real you, the you that you know is you, knows that struggle is just an old habit. The real you is the graceful, patient artist.

STEP 92: REVERSALS IN THE DEEP END

Let's review the feelings of being in the deep end. Each time you go there, start from the beginning. This cannot be emphasized enough.

- Feel what it's like to be in deep water, holding onto the side.
- Notice your breathing and your internal speed.
- Allow them to be as you find them.
- Stay in the deep if it sounds like fun.
- Feel what it's like to allow your body to dangle in the deep, face in. Naturally you're holding onto the wall.
- Feel the water holding you up.
- Ask yourself if you can depend on this feeling.
- Let yourself lie backward on the water, holding on. Review the back float at the wall.
- Feel the water holding you up.
- Ask yourself if you can depend on this feeling. Can you? How far down into your body have you gotten the belief, "I float in deep water?"

**Draw a circle to show how far down into your body
you've gotten the belief, "I float in deep water."**

Now, if it sounds like fun, stay in your body as you let go of the deep end wall. That doesn't mean letting go of the wall and taking a chance. It's something you learn by practicing the back float and reversal in the shallow end and in the deep at the wall (even though you're holding on, or with a tether), being in your body so consistently that you come to accept unequivocally that the water holds you up and that you'll remain in control there with ease.

It's now incumbent upon you to give yourself this practice without scrimping. Let it be the slowest practice you have ever done. If your pool session is typically 20 minutes, let it be 20 minutes of ultra-slow motion, internally and externally. Slow everything down even more than you have before.

If your energy is buzzing and you can't slow it down, so be it. Let yourself buzz. The back float and reversal back to the wall can wait for another day.

When you have practiced the back float and the reversal in the shallow water until you know beyond a shadow of a doubt that you can remain in control of it in the deep, then you'll look forward to it. It'll be safe to do it in the deep. Tell a lifeguard that you're doing it in the deep for the first time and ask him/her to keep an eye on you. If it makes you self-conscious, bring yourself back into your body. Stay true to yourself.

STEP 93: WHEN YOUR "ENGINE" IS IDLING TOO HIGH

Sometimes when you get into the pool, you're buzzing from your day. Your intention is to practice but you notice that you're vibrating so fast that you can't calm down. You're speeding inside.

A useful analogy to this is an unruly car of days gone by—a car whose engine was revved up too high at an intersection. The engine was working too hard and it made a lot of noise.

The cure for this annoyance was to use your foot to punch the accelerator quickly toward the floor and then let go so that the engine would race still higher for a moment, and then drop down to normal.

If your "engine" is idling too high and you try to practice a skill on top of that internal speed, it's easy to fly out to the 3rd Circle. Do not put yourself in this position. Catch yourself outside of the 1st Circle. Feel the speed—the tension. When you feel the tension and allow it, it can begin to let go. If you continue to allow it, it will let go completely.

If it is not disappearing as soon as you'd like it to, tense up more on purpose and hold onto this increased tension for awhile. Then let it go. You will drop down to a speed much slower than you were at previously. Doing the skill is not the goal, remember. Being in the 1st Circle is. Practice it.

Throughout this book we have been talking about how to be in control of your location. Now you're learning how to be in control of your speed.

STEP 94: THE CURE FOR "TOO MUCH:" BUILDING INFRASTRUCTURE

When your washing machine has an unbalanced load and all the weight is on one side, the machine spins unevenly, vibrates too much, sometimes wanders a few inches across the floor, and eventually shuts down. It can't function with that much vibration. It can't handle that much energy.

When a new freeway overpass is built, rebar is placed inside the cement— metal bars that give it added strength. The rebar enables the cement to withstand higher amounts of weight and vibration. Rebar is even more important in an earthquake. The more rebar, the better the overpass can withstand all the energy that passes through it. Rebar adds strength and flexibility to the overpass.

When you and I are having an easy day, we are comfortable whether we have a lot of "rebar" built inside us, or not. But when things get stressful, the more "rebar" we have, the better we respond.

I call this "rebar" *infrastructure*, mentioned early in the book. Infrastructure is lines of energy within our bodies, lines that we don't yet have instruments to measure but which are there and give us our ability to stay in control. These lines of infrastructure allow us to withstand large or even huge amounts of energy flowing through us, and still remain in control. Our "washing machine" won't shut down with an unbalanced load.

Some people have huge amounts of infrastructure—at least under certain circumstances. You'd expect a doctor to have plenty of infrastructure for the sight of blood, but the same doctor might be scared half to death in deep water.

Wouldn't it be great to have tremendous infrastructure in all situations? We can build infrastructure purposefully.

Situations that test our infrastructure can be as small as being called a name when we were children. That could pull us off our center and cause us to go out of balance. We may not have responded the way we wished we did.

A weightier situation could be feeling your feet sink when you're trying to learn to float and thinking, "I'm sinking," then scrambling to save yourself. The situation can be anything stressful. The more stressful it is, the more infrastructure you need to remain centered and in control.

What Builds New Infrastructure?

- Infrastructure is confidence.
- Confidence is a solid sense that you're safe.
- Feeling safe in water comes from being in control of yourself; having a choice about what to do.
- Being in control of yourself comes from being in your body, in the 1st Circle.
- Being in the 1st Circle allows you to be successful.
- Success builds confidence. Success builds infrastructure.

Put yourself into a situation where you'll be successful with your learning. Make it easy for yourself to succeed.

STEP 95: BOBBING WITHOUT USING THE BOTTOM

Bobbing is the act of bouncing in the water and coming up to get a breath. Doing it just once is called one "bob." Earlier you learned the chair toy and bouncing off the water. Let's review these. Use a nose clip. Hold your breath for this first exercise. "Sit" in a chair position with your feet on or near the bottom in shallow water. Take a small to medium breath so that you can "sit" with your face below the surface. If you're fairly buoyant, your face will be above the surface, which is fine. Extend your arms at shoulder height, just below the surface, and push downward on the water, sweeping down with your "paddles" (pancake palms) and the inside surfaces of your arms. This raises you out of the water.

Your sweep pushes you up, above the surface. Then, once you rise as high as your sweep takes you, gravity takes over and you drop back below the surface a few inches. Four inches? Eight? You bounce off the water at the imaginary line where gravity loses its force and buoyancy takes over.

Wait for this to happen. You begin to float back toward the surface without effort. As you approach the surface, and you get a sense that it's time to push down, sweep downward again with your arms and hands. This will take you up so that your face is in the air. You're holding your breath. No exceptions.

Do this many times until you can rely on the fact that the water will push you back to the surface and your arms will bring you above it. Come to be completely in your body for this up and down movement through the water. See how much work the water does, and how little you need to do to come up. If you're a sinker, you'll have to use more than one arm pull to return to the surface. You need not hurry.

When you have that down (and only when you have it down), add an exhalation to the end: on your way up toward the surface, just before you come into the air, forcefully expel your air. Since you'll be wearing a nose clip, you'll exhale through your mouth.

Once your air has been forcefully expelled there will be room in your lungs to receive a new breath. If you do have room in your lungs, go ahead and take a *comfortable* breath when your head is above water. You don't want to take the biggest breath that will fit.

Just do one of these bobs at a time for now. After each one, regroup, then do it again. Do it many times.

Bouncing off the water as you bob.

When you've learned a skill like this, it's a milestone. Give yourself rest time afterward to absorb it. Acknowledge yourself for a huge win!

STEP 96: MORE TOYS

HANDSTAND

Knowing what you know now, can you do a handstand in the water? It's easier to do this in water than on land. It's easier in chest-deep water than in three feet of water.

As always, the first priority is to remain in control. Maintain comfort for your nose: use a nose clip. The game is to get your weight lined up vertically over your hands so that your weight drives your hands to the bottom and keeps them there; place your hands on the bottom of the pool with your torso aligned vertically over them.

How do you get your hands to the bottom and keep them there? Experimenting with this teaches you about buoyancy, balance, and how the water works.

First, drive your hands to the bottom. Start in a front float. Kick both feet down at the same time so that your hips come up. Bend severely in half at the waist. You will be driven toward the bottom. Experiment.

Here are three steps to a handstand. Finding your way may look different.

One	Two	Three

Just have fun with handstands. The point isn't necessarily to do it: it's to learn about moving your body in the water. With play, you'll get it.

The end result. Your arms could also be straight and your palms flat. Getting your weight directly over your head is the main point. Arms and hands are just details.

SOMERSAULTS

A good toy for teaching yourself about balance and propulsion in the water is the somersault. Have you done one on land? If not, no problem.

As with all our other toys and skills, please let go of whether or not you do a "sommie" today or this week. The most important thing is learning about balance and presence. Take it easy.

Wear a nose clip. Tuck yourself into a ball, drawing your knees and head together: keep your knees and head very close together the whole time.

In a ball, head and knees close enough together.

Somersault.

Turn yourself with your arms. Place your hands behind you, palms facing the floor. Your arms/hands are your propellers. Sweep forcefully toward the

297

bottom, then forward with both arms/hands. Churning your propellers in large powerful circular sweeps from your shoulders, turn yourself in a 360. Chin tucked.

If it doesn't work, check to see if you're doing these two steps: tuck and churn. It's common to come out of a ball, which makes a sommie nearly impossible. You may need to slow down drastically and just focus on staying in a ball.

If it still doesn't work, try again, focusing on your head position. If your head isn't aligned with your spine, you'll turn sideways. Doing this over a black line on the bottom and following it helps.

Take your time. If there's a point at which you feel disoriented—if you and your body are out of sync—abort the sommie and return to the 1st Circle. Churn only as long as you feel in control. Then stop and stand up. It's okay to just go partway around and stop. If you do, you'll float back to the starting point.

Give yourself time to learn this. Remember, it's the journey that's most beneficial in the long run rather than completing the somersault. These games are helping you learn oneness with yourself, your body and the water.

When you master this, and other skills in this book, give yourself—or better yet, ask for—a STANDING OVATION. You certainly deserve it.

CLOSING YOUR EYES

Often people say they feel more sensations with their eyes closed.

FEELING MORE IS A GREAT THING

When you feel more, you get more feedback from your body. If closing your eyes is frightening, then of course, it's not time to do it. You could take an intermediate step, by closing one eye. Or, close your eyes halfway. Do what's fun.

When would you want to try closing your eyes? When you wish to build confidence in your skills. First learn the skills in the shallow end with eyes open. They practice them with eyes closed to understand them better.

Spend time feeling your floats, your turns (the ball), reversal, and games, with your eyes closed. Get your feedback from feeling rather than seeing. This builds your presence for each skill.

STEP 97: KNOWING WHERE THE SURFACE IS

When you roll from back to front and front to back, you need to know where the surface is so you'll know when to open your mouth for a breath and when not to. If you're in your body, you'll know. If you have been taking on water, practice this more slowly.

Roll over using a nose clip, and do it so slowly that you can pay attention to where your face is.

Be sure that your:
- 1st priority is to stay in control.
- 2nd priority is to keep your face and breath comfortable.
- 3rd priority is to roll over.

Once you agree with these priorities, you can pay attention to where the surface is. Do you see why it's important not to skip any steps?

Before you roll, notice where the surface is relative to your head and face. As you roll, feel your face as it moves past the surface, an inch at a time. Be in your face.

Practice this over and over. When you know your face is in the air, you'll know it's safe to open your mouth and take a breath.

When you want to do this without a noseclip, exhale slowly through your nose from the moment you start turning from front to back until after your nose arrives in the air to prevent water from entering your nose.

STEP 98: BOUNCING OFF THE WATER IN THE DEEP

When you have learned bouncing off the water in the shallow end, you'll know it so well that you may have the thought, "If I could do this in deep water, I could get air whenever I wanted it." True.

Being able to get air when you want it is the second most important skill to have. You can't get air when you want it unless you're in your body. That's why *being in control is* the most important skill. Do you agree?

If you haven't mastered the skill in shallow water, stay there and keep practicing it. With a tether, you could practice this in the deep.

REVIEW:

While bobbing, on your way back up you'll start to exhale to get rid of your air. The exhalation finishes as you come up through the surface. Now, there is room in your lungs to receive a new breath. Go ahead and take a comfortable breath while your head is above water. Again, don't take the biggest breath that will fit.

When you've practiced being in the 1st Circle and bouncing off the water in the shallow end—until you know beyond a shadow of a doubt that it will work in the deep—you may try it in the deep. Invite a lifeguard if that will help you feel safe.

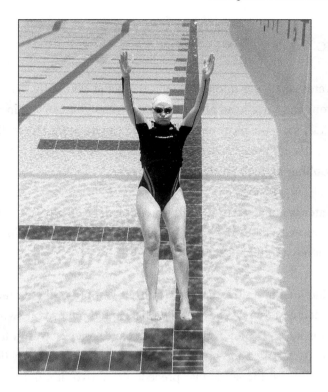

Do you need an intermediate step before trying it in the deep? Go to the deep end. Wear a nose clip. Float vertically. When you know that the water holds you up and that you can float near the wall holding your breath, practice bouncing off the water, but without the breathing. This is instructive (not to mention fun). Just sweep downward on the water, causing your head to rise above the surface. Let gravity take you back under. Let buoyancy and your sweep bring you back up. Feel what's happening. If you remain in your body and continue to practice this, something will eventually come to you: the breathing. If it doesn't come on the first day, trust it. It will come when you're in your body and ready. You can also go back to shallow water or crown-depth water and practice until this becomes part of you. Make it easy for yourself.

MELON DASH

TREADING WATER COMES SOON

Treading water is staying in one place in the water vertically, with your feet off the bottom and your head above the surface so you can see in any direction and talk. It's not the most restful skill you can do in the water; floating on your back is. It's not the easiest way to get air in deep water; floating on your back and bobbing/bouncing off the water are.

Treading water is not a safety skill. It's a convenience skill. To learn to tread, you have to already feel safe in deep water. If you don't, treading is unsustainable. You have to feel peaceful to learn it.

The skills that lead up to treading are far more important than treading itself and must be learned first. Treading, as well as breathing as you swim must be left out of this book. If they were included, eager readers would turn immediately to the back pages and read only those sections. Therefore, they would fail. When you learn the skills that precede these two, it's likely that you'll learn them without effort on your own. That's just the way it works.

By the time you reach this page, you will have made vast progress in your understanding of how to overcome your fear in water. *Standing ovation for you.* If you have not yet gotten into the water, the fun is yet to come. *Have a wonderful time.* Seal your book in a plastic bag and go. Don't expect to read it off the bottom: it will float to the top!

It is a noble step as an adult to learn to swim if you've had past failures. You didn't give up. Mazel tov!

Many students have said that taking this course has influenced their lives in many more ways than just learning to swim.

A fear manifested in swimming may underlie every other aspect of one's life. The possibility that learning how to swim could eradicate fear in other parts of my life was an eye-opener for me. —Corrie

Funny, since I conquered so much fear in these past two weeks, the world has opened up for me.—Mary (Age 71)

Hopefully, this book has provided you with ideas that have already caused shifts in your thinking. First and foremost, there's hope for you!

STEP 99: INVENTORY

Take stock of the beliefs and skills you have embodied, and those you still wish to own. Check the ones you *own*. This list serves, too, as a reminder of things to focus on and play with when you go to the pool.

BELIEFS

1. _____ It's safe to put my face in water.
2. _____ It's safe to go under water.
3. _____ It's okay to go at my own pace and not push myself.
4. _____ It's safe to walk to the middle of shallow water.
5. _____ I can stay in my body in shallow water for some things.
6. _____ The water holds me up in the shallow end.
7. _____ I know how long I can hold my breath.
8. _____ Shallow water is a safe place for me.
9. _____ I understand what staying in my body means.
10. _____ It's okay to be afraid in water.
11. _____ If I start to lose it, I trust myself to bring myself back.
12. _____ It's possible for me to have fun in shallow water.
13. _____ Swimming is not such a mystery anymore.
14. _____ It doesn't matter where the bottom is.
15. _____ I can stay in my body in shallow water, no matter what I do.

16. _____It doesn't matter where the side is.

17. _____I can get a breath when I need one.

18. _____I know which way is up and which is down when I'm in water.

19. _____It's okay if my feet go to the bottom when I float in shallow water.

20. _____The water holds me up in the deep end.

21. _____I am free in a pool.

22. _____I can be free in deep open water.

23. _____It's easier to learn to swim than I thought.

24. _____There's hope for me and my swimming.

SKILLS

I am comfortable with these skills. (not in any particular order)

1. _____getting into the water

2. _____walking in the water

3. _____putting one ear in water at a time

4. _____putting my ears in water

5. _____putting my face in water

6. _____relaxing my face in water

7. _____opening my eyes under water

8. _____smiling under water

9. _____exhaling through my mouth into the water

10. _____exhaling through my nose into the water

11. _____blipping (blowing out a few bubbles of air through my nose)

12. _____holding my breath under water

13. _____front float holding onto the side

14. _____back float holding onto the side

15. _____front float at the ladder (hands clasped behind it)

16. _____ front float with tether

17. _____back float with tether

18. _____ back float at the ladder (holding on loosely with one or both hands)

19. _____front float away from the wall

20. _____back float away from the wall
21. _____unfloating from a front float next to the wall
22. _____unfloating from a back float next to the wall
23. _____unfloating from a front float in the middle of shallow water
24. _____unfloating from a back float in the middle of shallow water
25. _____reversals
26. _____reversal and swim back to wall, shallow
27. _____reversal and swim back to wall, deep
28. _____swimming (propelling myself) on my back
29. _____swimming (propelling myself) on my front
30. _____jumping off the bottom
31. _____jumping into shallow water
32. _____getting out of pool in shallow water without a ladder
33. _____rolling from back float to front float
34. _____rolling from front float to back float
35. _____rolling 360 degrees (seal roll)
36. _____staying in my body as I approach the wall
37. _____buying a nose clip
38. _____using a nose clip
39. _____buying goggles
40. _____chair toy
41. _____knowing the difference between 6 hand positions
42. _____rising above the surface from chair toy with an arm sweep
43. _____descending a ladder and "taking the elevator" back up
44. _____swimming in the direction of my feet when I'm on my front
45. _____swimming in the direction of my feet when I'm on my back
46. _____swimming in the direction of my head when I'm on my back
47. _____swimming in the direction of my head when I'm on my front
48. _____being in my body
49. _____coming back to my body from the 2nd or 3rd Circle
50. _____not needing to return to my body because I didn't leave it
51. _____knowing where the surface is relative to my nose and mouth
52. _____whale jumps
53. _____turning 360s sideways

54. _____steering in different directions, whichever way I want to go

55. _____checking on my location to avoid bumping into something

56. _____going to the bottom in the shallow

57. _____going to the bottom in the deep

58. _____bobbing to get air, feet on bottom (shallow end breathing exercise)

59. _____bobbing to get air without using feet on the bottom

60. _____bobbing to get air in the deep

61. _____keeping water out of my nose

62. _____sitting on the bottom

63. _____standing on the bottom in the deep

64. _____vertical float

65. _____bouncing off the water

66. _____ball

67. _____being bounced as a ball

68. _____bouncing someone else as a ball

69. _____hopping

70. _____becoming balanced (after tipping)

71. _____squirting water from my mouth (not spitting)

72. _____swallowing under water with mouth closed

73. _____coughing under water

74. _____falling in from standing in the water

75. _____falling sideways

76. _____somersaults

77. _____handstands

78. _____sculling to give my body lift

79. _____rising from the bottom using 1 or 2 arm sweeps

80. _____rising from the bottom using just legs

81. _____gliding after I propel myself

STEP 100: FINALE

If you've learned the main message of this book—to stay comfortable all the time— your swimming has changed. Now, play (don't practice or work) with the steps for each of the ten fronts, until you master each one. If you follow the steps, you cannot possibly fail to become free in deep water!

If you've stayed in your body on purpose and tried anything in the book, you're forming an essential new habit that will lead to your freedom in water. Stay wet! If needed, you'll take breaks to catch up with yourself: sometimes the disbelief a person has about what they just did and the realization that they can do this skill need time to settle.

If you have done everything in this book and you stayed in your body, you may count yourself among the people who *can swim*. You've graduated! Standing ovation!

If by any chance, you feel unsuccessful, start again. Or, attend a Miracle Swimming course where you will be supervised in following the steps to a T. Everyone is a spirit in a body and therefore, The 5 Circles works for every-one, even if you disagree with it! Our teachers know how to use them and you just need to ask all your questions.

There is no doubt in my mind that the universal teaching in this book can succeed in healing any fear.

Go forth and be free.

"I got your message: Slow down. Slow down…no matter what I did.
Even if I did well. Slow down. And somewhere in the slowing down,
I got it!! I had tears of joy which were difficult to see in my goggles
(smile). But they were there." —Lakiba

APPENDIX

This section, Steps 64A-E, is a comprehensive recipe for overcoming a fear. If you feel that you're at fault for being afraid or for not being able to swim, or if the section on healing fear earlier in the book left you wanting, this is an important process to give yourself.

STEP 64A: HOW DOES FEAR HEAL?

HEALING FEAR IN STEPS

As mentioned previously, there is one important thing to bear in mind throughout: *fear is not your fault.* This section is for people who like to "dissect" things. It is very detailed. Take what you want and leave the rest.

Think of a friend, a family member, or even an acquaintance in whom you have complete trust. This is someone you trust as much as you trust yourself, holding him or her in the highest regard. We'll call this person Sue.

Let's say that Sue needs to borrow a car for the day, and she asks if she can borrow yours. You say yes. You're very comfortable with this. You have absolutely no qualms about it. You don't give it a second thought. As it turns out, she totals your car.

You trust Sue. You figure, "If she totaled it, chances are just as good that if I'd been in the same situation, I could have totaled it, too." You instantly and completely let her off the hook.

If Sue asked you the next week if she could borrow your car, you wouldn't think twice about it. You both might laugh. But you would lend her your car in a second because you still trust her. Your trust has not diminished.

Let's say that instead of Sue asking to borrow your car the second time, Joe asked if he could borrow it. You don't know Joe that well. You're unsure, but you let him borrow it, with reservations. Joe totals the car.

If Joe asked to borrow the car again, you probably would not lend it to him. You probably don't trust Joe anymore.

What's the difference between these two scenarios? Yes, you began with a different level of trust in the two people who borrowed the car. But that's not the operative factor. The important thing here is that you forgave Sue. Therefore, you're not afraid to lend your car to her again. You didn't forgive Joe. Therefore, you're afraid to lend it to him again.

IF YOU DON'T FORGIVE, A FEAR IS BORN

Fear is paralyzing but learning to forgive my fear had the opposite effect. I became courageous, in-control, a master of my life. After reading your book, I began to think about other fears that I had, and I addressed them, one by one.

I applied for a public service position in my small town. I started speaking in public, (so far, I've talked to over 300 people this year). I taught my daughter to drive; this was really scary. I purchased several pieces of real estate. I am leaving my job of 10 years at the end of June.

"Looking at fear from your point of view has really changed my life."
—Deborah

IS IT POSSIBLE TO LET YOURSELF OFF THE HOOK FOR WHAT HAPPENED THAT MADE YOU AFRAID?

If yes, you could skip the rest of this Appendix and return to Step 70. If not, read on.

WHY NOT LET OURSELVES OFF THE HOOK?

Check the truth of this statement for you. By not forgiving, we think we protect ourselves. We believe—before examining what we're doing—that if we forgive, we stand the chance of getting hurt again. We believe that we need to remain vigilant against the threat of this pain. This vigilance is fear.

No one does this consciously, I don't believe. It's our default mechanism until we become more aware. Who doesn't want to protect themselves from another hurt?

However, it works just the opposite way. If you forgive, you protect yourself better than if you don't forgive because without being afraid of being hurt again, you can be more present. You aren't divided against yourself.

If you forgive, you drop a burden.

1. If you forgive, and if something new happens that demands your full attention, you'll be present for it. You'll be able to feel the signals your body is giving you because you'll be in your body. On the other hand, if you don't forgive and you're still afraid you might get hurt again, you'll be thinking about avoiding the thing that happened last time. You'll be in the past, not the present.

2. If you forgive, you stand a smaller chance of being hurt long into the future by the original incident. For example, if you forgive Joe's totaling your car, then you won't carry the pain of holding it against him for years,

you won't dislike or mistrust Joe, you won't be afraid to lend your car to trustworthy people you could help, and you will then have the opportunity to be helped by them in return.

Before we forgive, there is pain. Can we acknowledge that? We grieve what we lost in the incident. You lost trust in yourself. This grieving is so worthwhile that we ought to have a holiday for it, in my opinion. Letting yourself grieve the loss allows you to put an error behind you. Consider this: if you don't grieve and forgive, the hurt will keep on hurting. For big hurts, this can last decades or even a lifetime.

Something happened that made you afraid in water. Perhaps:
- you were held under water by your older brother when you were both children, and you've been afraid in water ever since.
- your father threw you into a pool against your will and said, "Sink or swim! I learned this way and so can you."
- you were being carried into the waves on your mother's shoulders, she stepped into a hole, and both of you fell.
- your mother was afraid in water, and she told you that water is unsafe. Naturally, as a child you believed her.
- you were cultivating a tentative sense of security in water in high school but at a party your "friends" picked you up and threw you in, despite your cries that you couldn't swim.

In the first one, your brother thought it was funny to hold you under water, that you'd be okay, and he had no idea he was causing damage. In the second one, your father had good intentions: it had worked for him and he thought it would work for you. In the third one, your mother didn't know there was going to be a loss of control. In the fourth, your mother thought she was protecting you and herself. In the fifth, your friends were under the influence of each other's egging-on and may have known they were in the wrong. But they couldn't stop themselves.

In each of these scenarios, an innocent error was made. It was a purely innocent error, one made perhaps by you and perhaps one made by someone else. It's possible that an error was not innocent if made by someone else—but it probably was. Errors are innocent because they are caused by not knowing. Even if someone should have known better, they made the error because they let something overtake their better judgment. They didn't think about the consequences. Even meanness is an error. Let's figure out what the error was and use the steps to forgive it. If a fear was born, an error was not forgiven.

Perhaps you're saying, "I don't feel comfortable with the idea that I made an error." If this is the case, perhaps you're someone who has not been to the 5th Circle in the water. If you haven't, it's true, there may be nothing to forgive.

If you have been to the 5th Circle in water, please look closely. Something happened. You didn't know how to handle it. You did the best you could and you got through it, which saved your life! But in another way it didn't work for you. A judgment was made. That was the "error." It was such a purely innocent error that it fits the definition of *inno*: an innocent error you made that came from not knowing. Remove all the negative charge from "error," and you have "inno."

Look back to see when your fear in water began. What happened? What did you lose? If you can't remember how you became afraid, ask yourself where your beliefs about water came from. Finding out where you got your beliefs is a step toward healing. If you have no idea, it's okay.

Was there a situation you couldn't get out of? Was there a moment when you lost control? Was there a moment when you believed (perhaps not consciously) that you *had* to leave your body in order to get away from the pain? It may have been the single smartest thing you could have done at the time, but until now, you never looked at it this way. Was there a decision you made that you never wanted to repeat an experience, thereby limiting yourself in ways you couldn't know at the time?

When we make a decision that we never want to experience X again, we draw a line in the sand in one good way, but also in another not-so-good way. We can't know about that at the time. In this case, the decision has kept you safe, but now it's *not working for you because you haven't been able to learn to swim.*

What happened?

_____

_____

What did you lose?

_____

_____

Do you want to have compassion and understanding for yourself for not knowing how to handle the situation? Is there someone else to forgive as well? You don't have to forgive now. It's simply an accelerator for healing.

You may have thought that being held under water caused you to be afraid. Or that being thrown into a pool made you afraid. But these were only the circumstances, not the cause.

FEAR CAME WHEN YOU INNOCENTLY LEFT YOUR BODY TO AVOID PAIN, BUT DIDN'T FORGIVE YOURSELF FOR LEAVING.

In all situations that I have heard so far, if you abandoned your body instinctively in order to avoid pain, it seemed like the right thing to do at the time. And it was. Not that you had a choice about it! But it was understandable. Therefore, you wouldn't see a need to forgive yourself. Only now that you realize that leaving your body leaves it unprotected do you understand that you're safer if you stay, even if it's uncomfortable. Now you can see that leaving was an innocent mistake.

Who knew this was important?

On the other hand, it would be a different matter if you had said to yourself at the time, and this is highly unlikely, "They're throwing me into deep water. I'm going to leave my body so that I don't have to feel the pain (terror) of not knowing what to do and not having enough air." This would be an example of being in control of leaving your body. Since you would have done it on purpose, you would not hold it against yourself and no fear would have come from it.

ASK YOURSELF IF YOU WANT TO FORGIVE

Do you want to forgive yourself?

Yes _____ No _____ Maybe_____

Can you remember anything else that happened?

_____

_____

Whatever happened that made you afraid, and there are many more stories than the ones above, there are ten common denominators among all of the fear-producing incidents I have observed:
- There was a very painful experience.
- The person decided he didn't want to experience that pain ever again.
- He didn't know that by deciding not to experience that pain again, he would have to leave his body to prevent experiencing/feeling it if the situation arose again.
- The situation arose again.
- He left his body, just as he had unknowingly decided to do.
- By leaving his body he lost control of himself. He lost control of what his body did.

- He interpreted his loss of control as his being untrustworthy to take care of himself in that situation. He stopped trusting himself in that situation.
- He became afraid and decided to stay away from that situation altogether.
- He hasn't forgiven himself for leaving his body.
- He wishes he knew how to get over his fear.

Now, consider these:

- Do you agree that you believed that something was going to feel so bad you didn't want to experience it? Yes__ No__
- Do you agree that you made a decision, consciously or not, to leave your body if that situation arose? Yes__ No__
- Do you agree that you left your body next time the situation arose in the (unknown) belief that it was the best thing to do at the time? Yes__ No__
- Do you understand why you would leave your body? Yes__ No__
- Do you agree that you left your body not knowing that if you remained in it, you'd have more control? Yes__ No__
- Do you agree that you didn't forgive yourself for leaving? Yes__ No__
- Do you agree that you made a decision not to trust yourself in that situation any longer as a result of what happened? Yes__ No__
- Are you ready to re-examine your decision? It doesn't matter whether you make the same decision again or not—as long as you stay true to yourself. Yes__ No__ Maybe__

If you want to forgive, or if you're not sure, then first identify the inno.

The inno I made was: _____

It was innocent because: _____

The inno someone else made, if any, was: _____

Their inno was innocent because: _____

The decision I made as a result of the episode was:

_____

These are some big steps in this chapter. When you have completed this section, please give yourself a standing ovation—even if the healing is still in progress.

STEP 64B: HEALING UNFORGIVENESS

If I make an inno and I blame myself, blame acts like a wedge in me that keeps me out of my body. In other words, I unwittingly keep myself out of my body by not forgiving myself. Since I don't want to be out of my body, I can take steps to get back in.

Body, blame (wedge,) and myself

REMOVING THE WEDGE

1. Feel where the wedge—blame—is being held in your body. It shows up as tension. Where do you feel tension when you think about what made you afraid in water? Feel the tension now. Give yourself some time to sit with it. Don't be in a hurry: come to a stop.

Feel it and let it be there. It may feel like sadness. It may bring tears. This is good: "stuck" (contracted) energy is moving. If you distract yourself and start thinking about something else, that's okay. Just come back and feel it for as long as you want.

You may find it helpful to get in touch with the feeling by writing about it or recording it: what happened, who was there, how did it make you feel back then, how does it make you feel now, what did you want to say, what do you want to say now? What has the experience of becoming afraid in water cost you in your life?

By feeling the tension, the wedge, the pain, a teaspoon at a time (I'm not asking you to bite off more than you can chew) and letting it be there without trying to change it, it can begin to move. If you feel it long enough, it will change. It's as simple and certain as 2+2=4:

THIS IS A LAW OF LEARNING.

Occasionally in my classes, a student reaches tears. This usually means that something that's been "stuck" for a long time is moving. Sometimes it means that a belief has broken free: change is happening at its deepest level. It is most welcome.

It may take days or weeks or months to heal this wedge. It's time well spent. Think of how long your wedge has been there, costing you your freedom. "Months" to heal is quick! If you can let yourself sit with the tension of this wedge and feel it for a few minutes every day, taking breaks when you need them, you will, day by day, heal the cause of your fear. This causes a shift in your feeling, a shift in the tension held in your body, an increase in the freedom in your body. It's a physical event. Remember, an inner shift causes outer shifts:

beliefs → actions → experiences.

2. A second way to remove a wedge is to tell your story about how it came to be, many, many times. Tell it until it no longer holds one iota of pain for you anymore.

Find a person who is willing to listen to your story quietly and without judgment. He will not try to talk you out of your feelings. He will not try to "fix" anything. He'll simply listen with full attention and be neutral.

If this person gets tired after a number of repetitions, find a second person. Tell the person everything that happened to you. Leave out no detail. As you remember more, include it. Take your time. Talk about who was there, what was said, how you felt, what happened afterward, what you wish had happened, what it's cost you, and everything else you remember—even what the weather was at the time.

All that matters is that you feel heard and that you tell the story as many times as necessary until you have discharged the incident one hundred percent. The discharging of this memory is a gradual physical event. The complete discharge of it is a physical event that marks forgiveness. We don't know how long it will take, but we do know that if you stay with it, forgiveness will follow.

A PAINFUL MEMORY THAT LOSES ITS STING

While you're holding a wedge against yourself or someone else, or when you have pain left over from an incident, your cells carry an electrical charge that came from the incident—from a buildup of all the feelings that were not released or worked through the first time. This electrical charge is emotionally painful.

You can remove the charge your body has stored, as mentioned above, by feeling the emotions that still remain from the first experience a teaspoon at a time. If that doesn't sound fun, skip it.

You can also remove the charge by being gentle with yourself in the water and letting yourself be where you are. Little by little, the old feelings are replaced by new understanding of the water. Though you'll still remember that you once had a frightening experience, it will no longer have any power. You'll be free of it.

A representation of a painful memory stored in your cells:

The electrical charge of a frightening experience not yet healed. It's present in every cell of your body.

A frightening experience, healed. You remember that it happened, but the electrical charge is gone. It no longer matters. There is no more pain.

A painful memory stored (left) and discharged (right). ©M.Dash 1985

The same thing happens when you tell your story enough and feel the emotions, letting the stuck energy flow. The electrical charge goes away.

For forgiveness to take place, follow the steps and give yourself time. Just by beginning the process of overcoming your fear in water, forgiveness steps are being taken. To be reading this book is to have begun the healing process.

WE DON'T CARE IF YOU HEAL THE WEDGE.
WE ONLY CARE THAT YOU REMAIN
IN CONTROL, IN YOUR BODY.

As long as you remain in control, you're practicing staying in your body. You're enhancing your ability to remain in control in other situations. By the way, letting yourself cry about this is not losing—or giving up—control.

STEP 64C: PREVENT A NEW FEAR FROM SPROUTING UP

Here are two ways to prevent a new wedge from forming. There may be more.

1. When something "bad" happens, you need to decide how to interpret it. Will you blame yourself or will you use it as a positive learning experience? If you blame yourself, there will be an electrical charge left over, which, if left unexamined, will likely manifest itself in one of many ways. The sooner you feel the feelings and the emotional (electrical) charge, the less control this experience will have over you later. Correct me if I'm wrong, but I believe you don't want to carry this with you.

If you have a new experience of losing control in the water (you forgot to make the 1st Circle your #1 priority?) then when you come out of it, you may feel sadness, disappointment, confusion, fear, regret, anger, distrust, self-doubt, frustration, or more. It's best to bring your full presence to your feeling—to talk them through, write about them, soak in them and "milk them for all they're worth." Deal with your water episode exhaustively until you have wrung every last bit of energy from it. Take time. I daresay it's some of the most worthwhile time you will have ever spent.

If someone says, "Oh, just get over it," he is not helping you to heal. He is telling you to manage. If just managing fear were satisfactory to you, you probably would not be reading this book. You owe it to yourself to heal yourself. It's the only predictable way healing can happen. If you wait a few more years, there will likely be more to heal.

On the other hand, some people have indeed said to themselves, "I'm not going to hold this against myself, period." And it evaporated.

If you had an experience that made you afraid in water as a child and you have a fear of water today, you were unable to discharge the episode fully by talking, crying, and fully emoting. Therefore, you have leftover energy held in your body. If your parents did not ask you about it or allow you to explain what happened, enabling you to fully discharge it, then it's been building for years.

If we all had known this way back when, parents would have been more helpful in those situations, and many kids would not have grown up to be adults afraid in water. But since we didn't, at least we have the steps to follow now. It's not too late.

2. The second way to prevent a wedge (blame) is to interpret experiences in an empowering way. You have a choice about how to interpret a difficult experience. If you interpret it one way, you'll come away afraid. If you interpret it another way, you'll come away without fear, unscathed. Likewise, you've come away from many other experiences unscathed, while others who had those same experiences came away from them afraid.

After a scary experience, you can say to yourself, "This happened. It means that I cannot trust myself in this situation." Or, you can say, "This happened. There was something I didn't know about handling this situation. Just because I didn't handle it ideally doesn't mean I can't trust myself. It just means I need to learn what I was missing. I need to learn how to stay in my body if this happens again. I forgive myself for my inno. I still trust myself. And now I'll go and get the information I need."

WHAT HAPPENS TO A WEDGE THAT IS NOT REMOVED?

A wedge that is not healed meets one of several outcomes. A wedge, like everything else, can either expand or contract. The wedge expands if you contract—that is, if you do nothing, or tighten further. An expanded wedge puts more distance between you and your body, or you and someone else. We have all felt this distance or this increase in fear.

If the wedge goes through forgiveness, it gets smaller and fully heals. You expand. The distance between you and yourself or you and someone else disappears. We have all felt how good this feels, too.

If the wedge isn't healed, it festers. If it festers slowly, you may never see any effects from it. If there is a lot of charge left on it, you may notice physical effects. It may turn into a greater fear or a physical symptom, sometimes an injury, sometimes a dysfunction, sometimes an accident or illness.

STEP 64D: "DO I WANT TO KEEP THE WEDGE?"

You may think I'm crazy to ask such a question, but it's important. You may want to hold onto the wedge. This is okay. The important thing is to be in your body about it. Accepting where you are is a step of healing. For example: "I accept that I want to keep this wedge for now."

On the other hand, if you don't want to keep the wedge, you now have steps to heal it.

How does it serve you to hold it? If you're holding it, it must be serving you. If it weren't, you wouldn't expend this much energy to keep it. To hold it does not mean that you're a bad person, unenlightened, or doing a bad job. It simply means it's healing you in some way to keep it.

Do you have any thoughts about the wedge? Maybe it's protecting you. Check and see. It protects me by:

_____

_____

What would feel good?_____

HEALING FEAR IS ABOUT FEELING BETTER... AND, FINALLY, FEELING GOOD.

I hope you'll allow yourself to be right where you are in this process. You've done so much work already! Where you are is perfect and you are well on your way. You don't have to do it all yourself. Your goal will meet you in the middle.

TO SUMMARIZE THE HEALING OF FEAR

1. Fear is born when an inno is made and we don't let ourselves off the hook.

2. The reason we don't let ourselves or someone else off the hook for it is we believe that by not forgiving, we protect ourselves. Additionally, we have no idea how much it will cost us to hold onto it.

3. When we study the events of fear, we find that trusting protects us more than fearing and blaming.

4. When we study the events of fear, we find that there are simple steps to take that gradually and predictably free us from fear.

5. It is safer to be in the present than in the past. But we have to "work through" the past or let go of it.

6. When all is said and done, we learn that we truly are innocent.

STEP 64E: STAGES OF FORGIVENESS

How far down into your body have you come toward forgiving yourself for your inno?

The circles and descriptions below refer to a person's presence in the water relative to how much they have forgiven themselves.

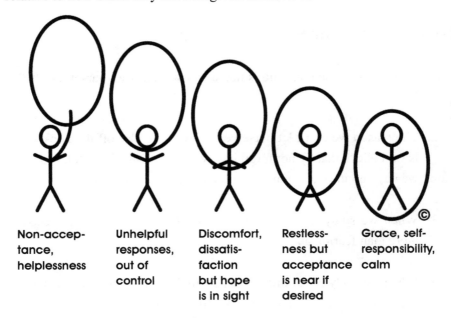

Non-accep- Unhelpful   Discomfort, Restless-   Grace, self-
tance,   responses, dissatis-   ness but   responsibility,
helplessness out of   faction   acceptance calm
            control   but hope   is near if
                        is in sight desired

**Our movement as we forgive. What circle are
you in with regard to forgiving yourself for a water mistake?**

How does fear heal? It heals two ways: by forgiving yourself and by changing your beliefs. The positive steps that you take in the pool help change your beliefs.

Forgiveness is obviously a process. What keeps us from forgiving? Fear. It's circular. Fear that if we forgive, we'll get hurt again. We can't control whether or not we get hurt again. To try to control this is to live a life in fear—so we may as well just trust and forgive—when it sounds like fun.

PLEASE RETURN TO STEP 65
PAGE 217

ABOUT THE AUTHOR

Melon (M. Ellen) Dash grew up in upstate New York and has been a competitive swimmer since the age of seven. She swam for four years at University of Massachusetts/Amherst, assistant-coached at several universities, and has ranked Top Ten in the United States in six events as a masters swimmer.

In 1983, she discovered that in order for afraid-in-water adults to heal fear, they must learn to remain completely present. She developed the 5 Circles Teaching Method on which she built her career, swim school, instructor trainings, books, and the Miracle Swimming Movement. Her hope is that it will transform swimming instruction and Education worldwide. Her U.S. Patent #11,331,554, Learn to Float Bar and Tether has ushered in a new era of adults learning to swim.

She resides in Sarasota, Florida. Her favorite toys are her Macintosh and her bike. She goes swimming and SCUBA diving whenever she can.

ACKNOWLEDGMENTS

First and foremost, many thanks to every student who has ever taken my courses—around six thousand of you since 1983—and the six in New Hampshire in 1978. They paved the way to all of the new knowledge in this book. Thank you to each of you who generously gave permission for your photographs, stories, and quotes to be included here.

I commend swim instructors who seek to serve students better. Highest kudos and warmest gratitude go to my students who have become instructors: Richard Schwarzenberger, Fred Peoples, Susana Mueller, and Jeannie Mariscal.

Many, many thanks to all the volunteers who have assisted in my work: the spotters, the video shipper, office assistants, and donors.

Many thanks also to each reader of the manuscript and to the survey respondents who informed this revision. Your enthusiasm and attentive feedback were invaluable! Each team of you and me—reader and writer—is a stepping stone to world water safety: the vast dissemination of this information to all. Together, we can end preventable drowning.

Highest respect to the late Harvey Jackins for his system of healing past hurts by discharging accumulated energy, Reevaluation Counseling.

The identification of swimming strokes as the choreography of swimming is attributed to Chris Canaday, instructor.

Lastly, I congratulate the adults who have not given up on learning to swim despite their past experiences; who know there must be a way to be successful, and who found their way to this remarkable answer.

Thank you for reading
Conquer Your Fear of Water
*A Revolutionary Way to Learn to Swim
Without Ever Feeling Afraid*

If you've enjoyed this book, please tell others by posting
a short review online on your website of choice such as
Goodreads.com, Amazon.com, librarything.com/,
https://www.lovereading.co.uk/, etc.

For more about Miracle Swimming books, classes, teachings,
and instructor training, visit:

miracleswimming.com
melondash.com
5circlesteachingmethod.com

If you have a question about overcoming fear in water that hasn't been answered in this book, feel free to ask it via the Contact form at
miracleswimming.com.

Index

Diagrams

A

B

C

D

E

F

T

U

V

W

CPSIA information can be obtained
at www.ICGtesting.com
Printed in the USA
BVHW052156240123
657059BV00011B/366